# PHILOSOPHICAL ISSUES IN ADVENTURE EDUCATION

## *Third Edition*

### *Scott D. Wurdinger*

**KENDALL/HUNT PUBLISHING COMPANY**
4050 Westmark Drive     Dubuque, Iowa 52002

Cover image courtesy of Corel Corporation.

## Dedication

*For my mother and father, Ramona and Don,*
*who have always encouraged me*
*to pursue my own adventures.*

# CONTENTS

# PREFACE

In 1972 my cousin talked me through my first rappel on a crumbly limestone quarry wall in northern Iowa. It made a lasting impression on me and was the beginning of a lifelong interest in adventure education. Those who have had similar experiences realize the power that an adventure can hold. Sometimes however, in our quest to expose others to adventure, we make generalizations that may not hold true for everyone. While writing this book I read numerous adventure program brochures that made such generalizations. In most cases the intentions behind these statements were probably good. Programs want to enhance self esteem, develop better leadership skills, and help individuals grow on a personal level. The problem is, they sometimes make assumptions that are inappropriate or inaccurate.

I wrote this book to point out some of these assumptions and to analyze their validity, so that the field can become more precise with its terminology. I also wrote it to encourage discussion on topics that in many cases are overlooked. If our field is to continue advancing academically and professionally then we must address important philosophical issues in adventure education.

# ACKNOWLEDGMENTS

I would like to thank my family for allowing me the time to pursue this project. My wife, Annette, gave me emotional and intellectual support by providing encouragement and valuable editorial comments; and my daughters, Madeline and Lauren, have provided constant unconditional love.

Dr. Jasper Hunt (Mankato State University) who has had a major influence on my thinking deserves a very special thank you. His mentoring gave me the inspiration and desire to overcome difficult obstacles which allowed me to complete this project. He examined my work on a number of occasions and provided important feedback on the philosophical components of the work.

I would like to thank several important people on the Ferris State University Campus. My Program Coordinator, Dr. Susan Hastings-Bishop, provided enthusiastic support and encouragement while finishing this edition. Dave Wininger from Media Distribution provided technical computer support which allowed me to format the book in a timely fashion. Jerry Sholl from Media Production took valuable time to scan and reproduce many of the photographs used in the book; and Jeffrey Ek, also from Media Production, provided computer support for the drawings.

Dr. John Tallmadge (Union Institute) and Dr. John Miles (Western Washington University) gave me important feedback on the earlier drafts of this manuscript. Their input provided me with ideas on how to link important historical authors to the philosophical underpinnings of adventure education.

I am also indebted to Dr. Tom Potter from Lakehead University for his thorough reading of chapter two which led to several important revisions. His comments were invaluable.

Dr. Mark Havens (Accessible Adventures) and Dr. Michael Gass (University of New Hampshire) provided fresh perspectives on how to package some of the chapter contents.

Many thanks go out to all the students from the adventure education programs at Ferris State University and the University of New Hampshire. They gave me ideas on how to make the book more useful and practical for students.

Lastly, I would like to thank long time friend and colleague Jeff Boeke, Director of Adventure Based Experiential Educators Inc. (ABEE), for his suggestions and comments concerning the overall flow of the book.

# INTRODUCTION

The concept of using adventure to enhance education can be traced back to the ancient writings of Plato, "Well then if risks must be run, should one not run them where success will improve people?" (1974, p. 128). In this quote from the *Republic*, Plato discusses the advantages of allowing the young to participate in risk-taking activities for the purpose of learning virtues such as wisdom and courage. This idea is foundational to adventure education and is still being practiced by numerous programs today.

Other foundational ideas were borrowed from early thinkers in the fields of philosophy and psychology. For instance, adventure education's learning process relies on Dewey's (1916, 1938) theory of experiential education, and the goal of building self esteem stems from Maslow's (1962) theory on self-actualization. Scholars continue to build upon and transform such ideas, which helps strengthen adventure education's theoretical foundation.

What is adventure education? In the context of this analysis it will be defined as a type of education that utilizes specific risk-taking activities, such as ropes courses and mountaineering, to foster personal growth. Its philosophy is built upon three basic tenets: using experience to enhance the educational process, building moral character, and developing a willingness to take risks (Hunt, 1990).

In adventure education participants often use an experiential approach which requires problem solving and active participation. They develop strategies to tackle a variety of hands-on activities. For example, on a mountaineering expedition students must master technical mountaineering skills, but they must also figure out which route to climb, how much food to bring, where to camp, and how to cooperate with their team. They gain knowledge and skill because they develop plans which are tested out in reality.

According to Coleman (1976) this process of learning is different than classroom learning. In classroom learning theory is often presented through lectures and discussions, and is then presumed to be applied by the student at a later time. In adventure education students are presented with a problem that requires hands-on participation and theory is then generated from the experience. This reversal in the learning process is one of the components that makes adventure education unique.

Another tenet is building moral character. Priest (1990) suggests that this takes place on two different levels. On an intrapersonal level the aim is to develop or enhance self esteem, and on an interpersonal level the goal is to develop or enhance social skills such as cooperation, communication, and compassion. Students are placed in groups and given risky, challenging problems that elicit group cooperation and build self esteem. This is why learning technical skills is secondary to building moral character.

A third tenet is developing a willingness to take risks. In adventure education emphasis is often placed on physical risk-taking such as climbing mountains, engaging in high element ropes courses, and camping in the wilderness. However, emotional risk-taking such as living with a group of strangers, exposing insecurities, and confronting someone in the group are also common to an adventure experience. Taking such risks is considered important because it not only helps people realize their true physical potential, but can help them overcome fears encountered in everyday life.

These three tenets can be found stated in one form or another in numerous program brochures. For example, "At Outward Bound you learn by doing, a process called experiential education," (Outward Bound Course Schedule, 1991, p. 3) asserts that adventure education is based on the experiential learning process. Such statements however, raise questions like how does experiential learning differ from other types of learning, and are adventure education and experiential education the same thing? Answering these questions is difficult and may require some philosophical inquiry.

Most of the research in this field however, is empirical in nature and supports the hypothesis that participation in an adventure experience raises self esteem. *A Critical Analysis and Review of Research of Outward Bound and Related Programs* conducted by Burton (1981) examined 72 studies which showed that Outward Bound and related programs have a positive effect on students. These studies used a variety of instruments, pre-tests, post-tests, and recordings of various observations to support this hypothesis. There is no doubt that this research is important because it helps us discover truths about the field, but philosophical analysis is important as well because it can help refine both theory and practice.

Philosophical approaches often examine questions that do not necessarily have one correct answer. For example, in determining what type of learning process is most effective, one can argue that theory should precede practice, or that practice should precede theory. Both learning processes have advantages and pitfalls which are important for educators to understand. Analyzing such questions requires that we think about our own views on knowledge, human nature, and morality.

At this point in time the literature in this field is lacking in philosophical examination. In fact, Miles and Priest, (1990) authors of one of the more comprehensive works to date state that, "practitioners are only beginning to explore the theoretical underpinnings of their work" (introduction). A review of literature over the past thirty years clearly reveals that there are only a handful of individuals who have examined certain philosophical issues in the field of adventure education.

One in particular is Crosby (1988), who analyzes the philosophy of experiential learning, and explains why this process is meaningful. She begins her discussion by pointing out the intimate connection between assumptions and their underlying implications and states that, "any theory (or action) of education is based on more general theories of epistemology, and those in turn are based on assumptions about metaphysics" (p. 74). This idea is important to my book because I too raise questions which have epistemological and metaphysical underpinnings.

Later in the article Crosby builds an argument based on elements contained in an adventure experience; challenge, support, feedback, and debriefing (p. 79). Challenge is the "felt need" to solve a difficulty or problem; support and feedback is information which tells us if we have resolved the difficulty or leads us into further perplexity; and debriefing is synonymous with reflection which helps us make sense of our experiences. This process is cyclical. First there is a challenge such as climbing a mountain that contains a variety of problems: what route to climb, how much food to pack, and what equipment to bring. Support and feedback tell us whether or not we have solved these problems and what we might do differently in the future. Debriefing is discussing and reflecting upon the experience. When reflection leads to new challenges, such as climbing a more difficult route or a different mountain, the cycle repeats itself.

Crosby suggests that this process leads to meaningful learning because learners are directly involved, and therefore, have an interest in completing the cycle. But, she doesn't raise questions such as what happens when there is no "felt difficulty", or no reflection? Implementing this process presents problems for the practitioner which Crosby does not discuss.

Her article gives credence to the experiential learning process, but it does not inform us about potential problems and pitfalls.

Wichmann (1988), on the other hand, challenges this learning process and warns his readers about the negative implications of experiential learning. In, "Babies and Bath Water: Two Experiential Heresies" he examines the similarities between the earlier progressive movement initiated by Dewey, and the later experiential education movement sparked by the formation of the Association for Experiential Education. He argues that both movements were initiated because of their reactions against the primary learning assumptions of formal education. This reaction took place so quickly that many failed to take the time to understand the theory before implementing it. The progressive education movement was providing experiences, but they were not necessarily educative ones, and eventually this faulty representation led to its death. Wichmann concludes that to be more successful than progressive education, experiential education must be more than reactive, and requires the following steps: "1) reexamine our present operations and theories in light of the learning-by-doing and reforming-by-doing fallacies, 2) develop a more sound theoretical framework based upon an understanding of historical and cultural alternatives and philosophies, and 3) provide for the ongoing empirical investigation of subject matter, methodologies, processes and outcomes" (p. 73).

Wichmann warns educators about mis-educative experiences and points out what the movement needs to do to stay alive, but he does not examine specific assertions which have theoretical underpinnings about experiential learning. Analyzing such underpinnings will help raise awareness about adventure education theory.

Drengson (1988) also examines the concept of experience and explains the value they provide to the learning process. He draws upon several historical sources to show that certain views lack essential ingredients necessary if meaningful learning is to take place. For example, he suggests that Hume's theory was lacking because it "was based only on inductive processes," and did not take into consideration other types of experiences (p. 88). Drengson's view is broader: "information does not become knowledge for us until we have made it our own..., until that is, we interact with it, relate it to what we already know, integrate it with our insights, and apply it" (p. 88). For Drengson, information cannot become knowledge until one experiences it and personalizes it. His article gives adventure educators another perspective of experience, but it does not examine what experiential learning means to adventure educators.

Crosby, Wichmann, and Drengson all examine experiential learning from slightly different angles, which is useful in helping educators understand this theory. However, the literature lacks a study which specifically examines what experiential learning means in the context of adventure education.

Another prominent individual who has provided the field with philosophical examination is Hunt (1990). In, "Philosophy of Adventure Education" he traces the developments set forth by individuals such as Plato, Aristotle, William James, and Kurt Hahn, and shows how their ideas have become some of the most important theoretical underpinnings in this field. He concludes that direct experience, learning virtue, and taking risks are the central themes.

James (1990) also traces the origins of adventure education by examining the life of Kurt Hahn. He argues that Hahn's ideas have become the underlying principles of Outward Bound: "But at its heart (Outward Bound), in every time and place, is Hahn's own center, his conviction that it is possible, even in a relatively short time, to introduce greater balance and compassion into human lives by impelling people into experiences which show them they can rise above adversity and overcome their own defeatism" (p. 12) Even though James limits his article to the life of Kurt Hahn, he is in agreement with the principles set forth by Hunt.

Richards (1991), however, suggests that Hahn borrowed some of his ideas from Plato. He states that, "Hahn was extremely clever at borrowing without copying," which may be the reason why Hunt and James arrive at the same set of principles (p. 68). He also points out that Hahn was unique because he was the first to bring these ideas together by using adventure as an educational medium.

Hunt (1990) also examines the nature of virtue in relation to practice. In "Ethics" he argues that in order for adventure educators to be virtuous, they must possess both intellectual virtue as well as moral virtue. The distinction between these two types of virtue is made clear by Aristotle who suggests that intellectual virtue is based on such things as practical wisdom, and moral virtue on such things as liberality and temperance (1962, p. 146). In other words, it is one thing for an adventure educator to know the technical skills required to climb a mountain (intellectual virtue), yet quite another to be patient with a slow climber (moral virtue). The ideas contained in his article are important because they examine the ethics of adventure education from a philosophical angle, yet have very practical applications.

A more extensive survey on ethics is Hunt's *Ethical Issues in Experien-tial Education* (1990). This is the only book in the field that discusses ethical theory and examines various ethical principles. Hunt draws from his philosophical background to discuss subjectivism, objectivism, and consequential and nonconsequential theories; but he also draws from his experience as an adventure educator to discuss pertinent issues such as, risk-benefit, informed consent, deception, secrecy, and captive popula-tions to mention a few. He ties philosophical concerns to practical con-cerns, and raises many questions for practitioners to consider. A similar approach will be used in this book.

An analysis of risk and human nature is also lacking in the field's lit-erature. James (1980), in "The Paradox of Safety and Risk," supports the use of risk by suggesting that it is a "countervailing force against the malaise of a society which has forgotten how to take risks," but he does not pull it apart and analyze how it effects human nature (p. 23). Priest (1990) also discusses risk, and gives us two different definitions. He claims that there is real risk which is inherent in reality and at times unavoid-able, and perceived risk is one's own view of an activity or situation (p. 116). Hunt (1990) also describes the two along the same lines only he refers to real risk as objective risk (p. 34). In both cases, Hunt and Priest give us workable definitions, but like James, they do not analyze its im-pact on human nature.

Finally School, Prouty, and Radcliffe (1988) have added to the theo-retical base of adventure education by writing *Islands of Healing*. This book, which is about adventure-based counseling, explains why certain concepts such as trust, risk, choice, and challenge are important to the healing process. It also helps people understand how adventure is used with therapeutic modalities. But, like most articles and books in this field, it does not analyze these concepts or show how they might be misrepre-sented in the field.

The works cited above were written with several different intentions. The articles written by Crosby, Wichmann, and Drengson examined the process of experiential learning, while the articles by Hunt, Richards, and James give us information on the roots of adventure education and the foundational tenets. Hunt also examined ethical issues which helped this field build a stronger theoretical foundation. Finally, Priest, James, and Hunt provided clarification and justification of risk, whereas Schoel, Prouty, and Radcliffe have given the field some guidelines concerning adventure-based counseling.

These individuals have provided a theoretical framework which must now be built upon by scrutinizing not only the learning process used in adventure education, but other philosophical underpinnings concerning risk, human nature, reality, and educational aims. In order to broaden the scope of understanding, a critique that examines the field's commonly held assumptions is necessary.

This field is filled with "doers." Many practitioners spend the majority of their time in the field providing people with adventurous experiences. While this may improve practice, it does not necessarily enhance theory.

The purpose of this book is to improve both theory and practice by examining a variety of philosophical issues in adventure education.

Chapter one identifies the foundational principles, and discusses their application to adventure education. It draws connections between the ideas of such philosophers as Plato, Aristotle, Rousseau, and Dewey and adventure education. All these writers discuss the educational importance of experience, risk, and moral development which are key elements that have helped build a solid theoretical framework. This chapter also discusses contributions made by the field of psychology. Freud, Erikson, Maslow, and Rogers have examined issues such as behavior, motivation, and trust that adventure educators have borrowed to further develop theory and practice.

Chapter two explains how to conduct a critical analysis which includes identifying and examining assumptions (Apps, 1985). This methodology was originally developed for the purpose of examining a field's theory and practice, however it can also be used to analyze underlying philosophical assumptions. A variation of Apps's critical analysis which includes: 1) identifying assertions that reflect the field's philosophy of education, 2) draw out assumptions that may contradict this philosophy, and 3) raise questions about these contradictions, is used to analyze assumptions in chapters three, four, and five.

It should be noted that many of the assertions chosen were taken from Outward Bound brochures, however ideas first stated by Kurt Hahn, the founder of Outward Bound, have since become foundational to the entire field. Therefore, this is an analysis of the entire field of adventure education

Chapter three analyzes the learning process. It points out that traditional methodologies are sometimes accused of using an inadequate process which is laden with theory and lacking in practice. Inversely, experiential methods sometimes overemphasize practice and exclude theory. The chapter concludes by suggesting that educators should work towards incorporating an appropriate amount of both theory and practice which will lead to more meaningful learning experiences.

Chapter four looks at risk and human nature. It discusses concepts such as perceived and objective risk, extrinsic and intrinsic motivation, and freedom. Certain assertions have a tendency to either misrepresent or devalue risk and human nature. Such misrepresentations need to be eliminated if the field is to build a stronger philosophy of education.

Chapter five discusses aims such as developing personal growth, transferring a learning experience from the adventure environment to another arena, and developing moral character. It points out that these aims may be misleading because growth, transference, and moral development are difficult to measure and assess. Furthermore, it appears as if certain programs are caught up in an advertising campaign that promises to provide individuals with life changing experiences. The chapter concludes by suggesting that the field should not be making promises that it cannot keep.

# REFERENCES

Apps, J. W. *Improving Practice in Continuing Education*. San Francisco: Jossey-Bass Publishers, 1985.

Burton, L. *Critical Analysis and Review of Research of Outward Bound and Related Programs*. Rutgers University: 1981.

Coleman, J. Differences between experiential and classroom learning. In M.T. Keeton (Ed) *Experiential Learning*. San Francisco: Jossey-Bass, 1976.

Crosby, A. A critical look: The philosophical foundations of experiential education. In R. Kraft and M. Sakofs (Eds.), *The Theory of Experiential Education*. Boulder: The Association for Experiential Education, 1985.

Dewey, J. *Democracy and Education*. New York: The Free Press, 1916.

Dewey J. *Experience and Education*. New York: MacMillan Publishing Co., 1938.

Drengson, A.R. What means this experience. In R. Kraft and M. Sakofs (Eds.) *The Theory of Experiential Education*. Boulder: The Association for Experiential Education, 1985.

Hunt, J.S. Ethics and facility-based adventure education. National Ropes Course Symposium, Pecos River, New Mexico, 1990.

Hunt, J.S. Dewey's philosophical method and its influence on his philosophy of education. In R. Kraft and M. Sakof (Eds.), *The Theory of Experiential Education*. Boulder: The Association for Experiential Education, 1985.

Hunt, J.S. *Ethical Issues in Experiential Education*. (2nd Edition), Boulder: The Association for Experiential Education, 1990.

Hunt, J.S. Ethics. In J. Miles and S. Priest (Eds.), *Adventure Education*. State College: Venture Publishing Inc., 1990.

Hunt J.S. The philosophy of adventure education. In J. Miles and S. Priest (Eds.) *Adventure Education*. State College: Venture Press Inc., 1990.

James, T. Kurt Hahn and the Aims of Education. *Journal of Experiential Education*. 1990, *13*, 1.

James, T. The paradox of safety and risk. *Journal of Experiential Education*. 1980, Fall, 20.

Maslow, A. *Toward a Psychology of Being*. New York: The Free Press, 1962.

Miles J. and Priest S. (Eds.) *Adventure Education*. State College: Venture Publishing Inc., 1990.

North Carolina Outward Bound brochure, Morganton: North Carolina Outward Bound, 1991

Outward Bound Course Schedule Brochure, 1991.

Plato, *Plato's Republic*. G.M.A. Grube (Ed.), Indianapolis: Hackett Publishing Co., 1974.

Priest, S. The semantics of adventure education. In J. Miles and S. Priest (Eds.), *Adventure Education*. State College: Venture Publishing, 1990.

Richards A. Kurt Hahn. In J. Miles and S. Priest (Eds.) *Adventure Education*. State College: Venture Publishing, 1990.

Schoel, J., Prouty, D., and Radcliffe, P. *Islands of Healing*. Project Adventure, Inc. 1988.

Wichmann, T.F. Babies and bath water: Two experiential heresies. In R. Kraft and M. Sakofs (Eds.), *The Theory of Experiential Education*. Boulder: The Association For Experiential Education, 1985.

# FOUNDATIONS OF ADVENTURE EDUCATION

To locate the roots of adventure education one may look in the fields of philosophy and psychology. Philosophers such Plato, Aristotle, and Rousseau; and psychologists such as Freud, Erikson, and Maslow all have ideas which are useful to adventure education. Many of these ideas have become foundational to the philosophy of adventure education.

Whitehead once said that, "The safest general characterization of the European philosophical tradition is that it consists of a series of footnotes to Plato" (1929, p. 39). In many respects this is true. The field of adventure education is no exception in that it uses several Platonic ideals to strengthen its theoretical foundation (Skidelsky, 1969; Kraft, 1985; James, 1985; Hunt, 1991).

In the article, "Philosophy of Adventure Education" Hunt (1991) discusses Plato's contributions to the field. One of these contributions is that direct experience is important to the learning process. "It seems obvious to Plato that the best way to learn about what one needs to know for one's maturity, is to experience it directly as a young person" (p. 120). This idea can be found sprinkled throughout Plato's Dialogues. For instance, in the *Theaetetus* Socrates states the following: "The reason of this is said to be that Artemis-the goddess of childbirth-is not a mother, and she honors those who are like herself; but she could not allow the barren to be midwives because human nature cannot know the mystery of an art without experience..." (1949, p. 9). In this passage Socrates uses the practice of midwifery as an analogy to the learning process and is asserting that experience is vital when it comes to claiming knowledge. This idea is foundational to adventure education because the learning that takes place is primarily through direct participation. When one experiences something first hand, the level of understanding deepens. In adventure education it is impossible to master the art of rock climbing without experiencing it. One can learn about the equipment used and how to tie the various climbing knots, but to truly understand and

know rock climbing one must engage in the practice. This is why Plato suggests that to know the mystery of an art one must experience it.

Adventure education programs such as Outward Bound and National Outdoor Leadership School continue to utilize Plato's idea of learning through experience, but their notion of experiential learning often means participating in risk-taking activities such as rock climbing, or kayaking. This notion may be one reason why the terms "experiential education" and "adventure education" are sometimes interchanged.

But learning through experience is a *process*, or one way in which we come to know ideas, whereas for adventure educators it is sometimes thought of as a *content* which revolves around adventure activities. Experiential education is a process of learning which can be used with a variety of subject matters: it is a theory which claims that experience is a vital component to the learning process. Adventure education may be thought of as a subset of experiential education because it utilizes this process, but there are many other subjects that use it as well. Sports activities and skills such as sewing, pottery, and painting require learning through experience. It is also used with more formal subjects like math and science in the form of labs, field trips, and internships.

A second fundamental idea which adventure education borrowed from Plato, is the importance of building moral character (Skidelsky, 1969; Hunt, 1991). In the *Republic*, Plato focuses on how to build a virtuous city and

# The Umbrella of Experiential Education

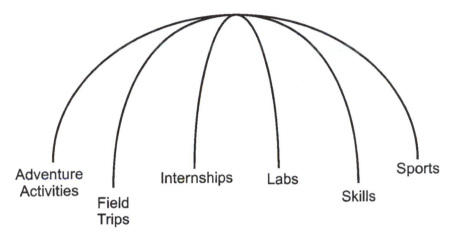

Figure 1.1 *Various forms of experiential education that require hands-on learning.*

concludes that, "each one of us likewise will be a just person, fulfilling his proper function, only if the several parts of our nature fulfill theirs" (1941, p. 139). For Plato, the individual is actually a miniature replica of the state and fulfilling our proper function means that we must rule our bodily appetites with reason, just as the philosopher king in the city state presides over the craftsmen and guardians.

This idea was first put into action when Kurt Hahn developed the first Outward Bound school, and Hahn's techniques have been widely imitated. However, adventure education's notion of developing moral character has diverged slightly from Plato's. The ends are the same, but the means are different. For Plato, virtue meant fulfilling one's proper functions, which in turn meant doing the job to which one was naturally inclined, and doing it well. This is how a virtuous city state operates. Adventure education, on the other hand, does not assume that there are only certain people who are naturally inclined to do well in adventure activities. Everyone can succeed in adventure activities if they try. Therefore, adventure educators are trying to provide all people with experiences that can help them become better people. In short, they are trying to provide adventurous value-forming experiences using adventure as a vehicle. This way students may become not only more productive members of their work community, as Plato intended, but also productive members of society as well.

A third idea contributed by Plato, is the importance of taking risks. "From Plato the argument is put forth that no, all danger should not be avoided; the use of danger is justified by making better people; and care must be taken to rescue the young people if too much danger presents itself" (Hunt, 1991, p. 123). This idea is best depicted in the *Republic* where Socrates and Glaucon discuss how the young should be raised.

*Socrates:* What you say is true, I said, but do you think that the first thing we should aim at is to take measures to avoid danger?

*Glaucon:* Certainly not.

*Socrates:* Well then, if risks must be run, should one not run them where success will improve people?

*Glaucon:* Obviously.

*Socrates:* And do you think that it makes little difference, and is not worth the risk, that the children, who are the future warriors, should observe matters of war?

*Glaucon:* No. It does make a difference with regard to what you are mentioning.

*Socrates:* We must then make opportunities for the children to observe war while contriving to keep them safe, and all will be well, will it not?

*Glaucon:* Yes.

*Socrates:* Well, said I, in the first place their fathers will know, as far as men can, which expeditions are dangerous and which are not.

*Glaucon:* That is likely.

*Socrates:* So they will take them on some expeditions, but be cautious about others.

*Glaucon: Rightly (1974, p. 128).*

From this passage it is clear that Plato believes it is important to take calculated risks in order to better ourselves. This central tenet holds that in order to learn and grow people need to step beyond their comfort zones. Through this process people learn more about themselves and the world in which they live. Risks take many forms, but in adventure education they are obvious and well defined. Hahn used adventure as a tool to get at the values inherent in taking risks. He saw it as a unique medium which actually allows people to experience intangible ideas such as courage and compassion.

These presuppositions — knowledge based on experience, the aim of moral education, and the importance of taking risks — are at the heart of adventure education. They are, taken together, what differentiate adventure education from other pedagogical methods.

Aristotle also contributed several ideas which the field of adventure education utilizes (Kraft, 1985; Hunt, 1991). According to Kraft, Aristotle's philosophy has influenced educators to use an experiential approach to education: "in the debates over educational practice, it becomes a question of emphasis, with experiential educators taking their cue from Aristotelian metaphysics and decrying the lack of experience on the part of young people today, who spend thirteen to twenty or more years in a formal school setting mastering theories which are often unrelated to the 'real' world for which that education is supposedly preparing them" (1985, p. 10).

Hunt (1991) expanded upon this idea by suggesting that Aristotle's philosophy fits well with adventure education because one must experience the virtues in order to learn them. In *Nichomachean Ethics* (Translated by Ostwald) Aristotle states the following: "It is by playing the harp that men become both good and bad harpists, and correspondingly with builders and all the other craftsmen: a man who builds well will be a good builder, one who builds badly a bad one. The same holds true of the virtues: in our transactions with other men it is by action that some become just and others unjust, and it is by acting in the face of danger and by developing the habit of feeling fear or confidence that some become brave men and others cowards" (1962, p. 34).

This idea is similar to Plato's in that one must be exposed to risk-taking situations in order to learn how to act courageously. But for

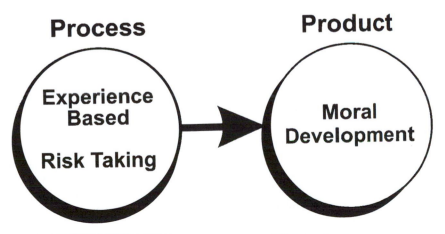

**Figure 1.2** *The theory behind adventure education.*

Aristotle it is the action, not the idea, which helps develop habits, and virtue is a habit that must be practiced.

Adventure education embraces this idea by placing a strong emphasis on practice. In order to become more virtuous, one cannot just sit around and discuss ideas on how to become virtuous, one must go out and experience it first hand. People understand things better, and become good at doing different things by practicing them. Habit in the traditional sense means something fixed or routine, but for Aristotle it meant perfection, and therefore, in order to perfect virtue one must practice doing good things over and over.

Another foundational Aristotelian idea centers on choice. "In general, choice seems to be concerned with the things that lie within our power" (Nichomachean *Ethics* 1962, p. 59). This section discusses the role choice plays in making decisions. According to Aristotle, we must deliberate carefully about the things which lie within our power so that right decisions can be made. Adventure education uses this idea when it places individuals in problem solving activities that require careful deliberation. In fact, Project Adventure, a well known program, has adopted the slogan "challenge by choice" to assert that deliberation is an important element in the learning process. In this sense, the meaning of choice is very similar to Aristotle's notion, but adventure education has taken it a step further by stating that choice is the first step towards a meaningful learning experience. Adventure educators believe that in order for meaningful learning to occur students must determine that they want to participate, otherwise the activity is forced and may result in no learning at all. Therefore, choice is an important element not only in the midst of the adventure, but at the very outset as well.

Another philosopher who has influenced the philosophy of adventure education is Jean Jacques Rousseau. In fact Kraft suggests that, "the experiential education movement can trace its roots back to Rousseau's *Emile* or to the Progressive Movement of the 1930's in this country" (1985, p. 7).

One of Rousseau's ideas, which is found in adventure education literature, is that learning through experience in a natural setting is important. In *Emile* he states that, "If he knows nothing by heart, he knows much by experience. If he reads less well in our books than does another child, he reads better in the book of nature" (1979, p. 160). Rousseau wanted Emile to be outside where he could run, play, discover, and experience things first, before learning to read. In fact, he kept Emile away from "book learning" until late in his adolescent years.

Learning through experience in the outdoors is also at the heart of most adventure education programs. Mountains and rivers are often used as classrooms, and learning takes place through a variety of wilderness excursions. Rock climbing and mountaineering courses take place in the mountains, and canoe and kayak trips take place on rivers and lakes.

Even though Rousseau and adventure education hold much in common they diverge when it comes to using the urban environment as a classroom. For Rousseau, the city was filled with vice and was a place where children learn the evils of life. Adventure educators, on the other hand, are beginning to realize that urban environments provide unique risk-taking opportunities. For many, the city is an unfamiliar environment that offers a variety of learning experiences. This is why organizations, like Outward Bound, are taking their programs into the city. And even though the majority of adventure education still takes place in wilderness settings, adventure educators are tapping into the urban environment where most of the population lives and works.

Another of Rousseau's ideas, which is still common in the field of adventure education today, is that physical exercise leads to the development of a healthy body and a sound mind. "Thus, the more his body is exercised, the more his mind is enlightened; his strength and his reason grow together, and one is extended by the other" (1979, p. 118). This concept is central to many adventure education programs throughout the United States. Programs which offer adventure activities, such as mountain climbing, require a certain amount of physical endurance from their students. Some programs even have students running mini-marathons. The purpose of such activities

is not necessarily to promote competition, but to push students physically, which will in turn push them mentally and enhance their ability to overcome the stresses of life.

Rousseau also held that education requires both doing and thinking, often in that order. "To learn to think therefore, it is necessary to exercise our limbs, our senses, our organs, which are the instruments of our intelligence" (1979, p. 125). The field of adventure education agrees that learning is often more meaningful when the doing comes first. In adventure education the doing phase often involves physical movement for the purpose of mastering certain skills. The doing phase is then followed by reflecting upon what was done and why it was done. In a sense, adventure education has taken the traditional western learning process and turned it on its head. This is because hands-on experience stimulates the thinking process.

In *Emile*, Rousseau argued that this process was a natural fit for younger children. Children are more inclined to run and play than they are to sit and be passive. Book learning comes later in Rousseau's educational scheme. Adventure education agrees with this idea, but has broadened its application to include all ages. Human beings are active creatures-they do not like to sit passively for long periods of time and listen to someone dole out information. Adventure educators believe that people would rather take this information and put it to some use, thereby testing it in real life situations and drawing their own conclusions. In adventure education, a structured and intentional process helps people experience an activity and draw meaning from it. The information learned from the experience is not dictated by a book or another person, but is assimilated and synthesized directly by the individual.

Dewey has also contributed much to the theory of experiential learning, and therefore, the field of adventure education (Kraft, 1985, 1991; Wichmann, 1985; Crosby, 1985; Hunt, 1985, 1991). He built his philosophy based on a dynamic view of knowledge. In *Democracy and Education* (1916), one of his earlier works, you can hear echoes of Plato's *Republic*, and Rousseau's *Emile*, but Dewey believed that these two individuals built educational systems based on static ideals.

> *But progress in knowledge has made us aware of the superficiality of Plato's lumping of individuals and their original powers into a few sharply marked off classes; it has taught us that original capacities are indefinitely numerous and variable. It is but the other side of this fact to say that in the degree in which society has become democratic, social organization means utilization of the specific and variable qualities of individuals, not stratification of classes. Although his educational philosophy was revolutionary, it was none the less in bondage to static ideals (p. 90-91).*

And later he states that Rousseau's philosophy is antisocial, and does not lead to educational growth.

> *"Nature" still means something antithetical to existing social organization; Plato exercised a great influence upon Rousseau. But the voice of nature now speaks for the diversity of individual talent and for the need of free development of individuality in all its variety. Education in accord with nature furnishes the goal and the method of instruction and discipline. Moreover the native or original endowment was conceived, in extreme cases, as nonsocial or even as antisocial. Social arrangements were thought of as mere external expediments by which these nonsocial individuals might secure a greater amount of private happiness for themselves (p. 91).*

Rather than educate the individual solely for the individual's own sake, as Rousseau suggests, or educate the individual primarily for the purpose of enhancing society, as implied by Plato, Dewey believed that we should educate the individual by "widening the area of shared concerns, as well as, for the purpose of liberating greater diversity of personal capacities" (1916, p. 87). According to Dewey these two elements must be present in education, otherwise it becomes static because no new ideas can enter the system. We need contact with groups of individuals so that we can broaden our own personal ideas. Without this contact, personal diversity

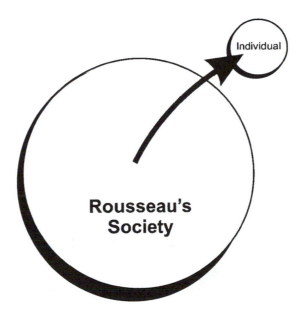

**Figure 1.3** *Rousseau's vision of education was to remove the individual from society and educate for the sake of the individual, not society.*

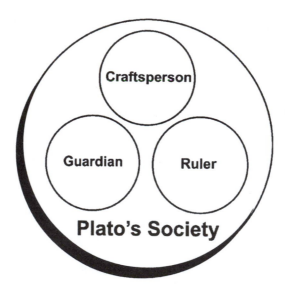

**Figure 1.4** *Plato's vision of education was to educate the individual for the sake of improving society.*

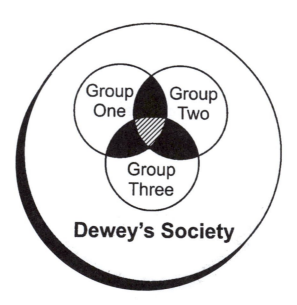

**Figure 1.5** *Dewey's vision of education was to educate Individuals to promote personal growth which would lead to greater diversity in Society.*

becomes limited, as does the area of shared concerns. Eventually, if this were to continue, individual growth, and growth within the community, would cease.

This view of education has led to the assumption that participation and cooperation are important to the experiential learning approach utilized in adventure education. Building group cohesiveness is one of the primary aims in adventure education. In this field instructors often contrive activities so that individuals must work together as a group in order to solve particular problems. This leads to a sharing of ideas while working towards a common goal. From these experiences people learn that it is often easier and more efficient to work together rather than individually. They also realize that diversity contained within a group not only broadens individual perspectives, but can be used to their advantage while solving various problems.

Another common thread running throughout much of Dewey's work is the need for experience in education. This theme is clearly depicted in such statements as: "In what I have said I have taken for granted the soundness of the principle that education in order to accomplish its ends both for the individual learner and for society must be based upon experience-which is always the life experience of some individual"(1938, p. 89), and "An ounce of experience is better than a ton of theory simply because it is only in experience that theory has vital and verifiable significance" (1916, p. 144).

Experience, for Dewey, was the quintessential element of education. Although Plato, Aristotle, and Rousseau all mention this concept in their writings, Dewey pulls it apart and looks at its elements. Thus he arrives at a broader and fuller definition of experience, which has since been adopted by the field of adventure education.

According to Dewey, experience involves a cyclical process which has an active and a passive phase. The active phase involves trying or experimenting and the passive entails reflecting upon what was done. If reflection does not take place, then according to Dewey, it is a blind experience. For example, if an adventure education instructor runs a course in the same fashion every time, simply walking through the same motions, and does not take past experiences into consideration, then he or she is not learning. One must take past experiences and apply them to future experiences in order for learning to take place. Dewey makes this clear when he states that: "Experience as trying involves change, but change is meaningless transition unless it is consciously connected with the return wave of consequences which flow from it" (1916, p. 139).

Furthermore, he believes it is important to take experiences from one setting and apply them to another. In a critique of formal schooling Dewey mentions that, "It is to emphasize the fact, first, that young people in traditional schools do have experiences; and, secondly, that the trouble is not the absence of experiences, but their defective and wrong character-wrong and defective from the standpoint of connection with further experience" (1938, p. 27). We can gather from this passage that Dewey wanted students to have classroom experiences which could be applied to experiences outside the classroom.

This idea is central to many adventure education programs. They recognize that experiences must be of a quality which can be applied to other areas of life. For that reason, adventure education programs have developed various experiences which require taking risks, working in small groups, or solving problems. These skills can be readily used in a variety of situations unrelated to adventure education, and the goal is to learn and practice them for future application.

Another idea, introduced by Rousseau and developed by Dewey, is that individuals cannot be forced to learn. For learning to be meaningful, the motivation must come from within the individual. External force only works to control behavior, it does not work to control the learning process. "In the strict sense, nothing can be forced upon them or into them. To overlook this fact means to distort and pervert human nature" (Dewey, 1916, p. 25).

This idea has led to the assumption that in order for an experience to be meaningful individuals must not be forced to participate in an activity. Self initiation is the first step towards a meaningful experience. It gives freedom to the learners to determine, not only participation level, but what is to be learned from the experience. The individual is in control of his or her own learning, and determines what is of most interest and value. When individuals are forced to participate they sometimes resist, or may feel captive and obligated to learn what the instructor wants them to learn. Productive learning will surely go awry when self initiation is eliminated. This idea adds strength to the commonly held assumption of choice, and has become an integral part of the philosophy of adventure education.

Plato's, Aristotle's, Rousseau's, and Dewey's theoretical ideas can be found trickling throughout adventure education literature. Over time, these individuals expanded upon the ideas of their predecessors, and in so doing, have added greater depth and meaning to the field of education as a whole. In adventure education they have helped clarify goals, make sense out of educational practices, and helped build a strong theoretical foundation. Individually, these ideas are powerful. Educational innovators like Kurt Hahn brought them together in a new way and created a new educational approach-adventure education.

This new approach however, was based on some of Plato's fundamental principles (Skidelsky, 1969, James, 1985, Richards, 1990). In fact, Hahn was so intrigued with the concepts outlined in the *Republic* that he designed a school modelled on these principles (Skidelsky, 1969; James, 1985). Even though this particular school never came to fruition, Hahn did not lose sight of this goal and later implemented some of these ideas when he founded the first Outward Bound school.

The Salem, Gordonstoun, and Outward Bound schools were all based on the notion that educating for the purpose of building moral character was just as important as training the intellect (James, 1985). For Hahn, "effective leadership meant developing personal attributes such as, courage, humanity, compassion, resolution and moral strength" (Skidelsky, 1969, p. (188).

The goal of developing these attributes was not new to the field of education, but the way in which Hahn developed such character-building traits was new. Hahn would send people out on extended mountaineering and sailing trips for the purpose of enduring physical and mental hardships, which in turn would not only help individuals develop a strong sense of self but a strong sense of courage and compassion.

Building moral character by participating in adventure activities is still one of Outward Bound's main goals. Their schools, as well as those of numerous other adventure programs, have students participating in activities such as ropes courses, rock climbing, and kayaking for the purposes of developing better social skills and enhancing self esteem. Adventure is only the medium which aims toward the greater goal of character development. Although the roots of this idea extend back to Plato, Hahn must be credited for using adventure activities such as mountain climbing and sailing for the purpose of enhancing social skills and moral development.

He also used the idea that providing service to others promotes moral development. In *English Progressive Schools*, Skidelsky (1969) discusses some of Hahn's ideals upon which the Salem school was based. One such idea was that, "The training in leadership was a cross between the public school prefect system and the idea of service to others..." (p. 193). Providing service to others was important, not only because it promoted a community atmosphere, but because it also helped individuals become more well-rounded.

Older boys, for example, more adept at certain skills, were required to help the younger and less experienced boys. This meant that in the process of learning virtues such as patience and courage, individuals had to undertake actions which they might ordinarily avoid. Hahn would take the "bookworms and encourage them to engage in practical activities; and take the practical students and introduce them to the joys of the intellect" (1969, p. (194). He was also known for turning extroverts "outside in" and introverts "inside out" (p. 93). For Hahn, the process of providing service to one another, as well as participating in numerous and varied activities, was crucial for developing moral character.

Finally, Hahn incorporated into his programs the idea that demanding physical exercise builds character. "The objective of the course was to build character by putting boys through testing physical experiences" (Skidelsky, 1969, p. (194). Endurance activities such as mountain climbing and sailing, which require physical strength and stamina, were the primary activities used at the first Outward Bound school. Hahn used these activities to test physical limits, which in turn helped develop such attributes as perseverance and confidence.

We can hear echoes of Rousseau in this statement, but for Hahn the course with its physical elements was not just a way in which to build a strong mind. According to James (1985), Hahn saw it as a way to control their activities, "From Salem onward he woke his students early, exercised them, controlled their activities. Even their time to relax and their time to be alone were strictly regulated" (p. 43). Hahn argued that by structuring their activities he could safeguard them from becoming lazy and apathetic. Group exercises and activities provided a way to promote proper social behavior and citizenship.

This view is still central today to many adventure programs. Many adventure courses are filled with nonstop activities which require a fair amount of physical exercise. Activities are both physically and mentally challenging, and promote endurance, motivation, and self esteem.

The field of psychology has also made contributions which have helped create and strengthen the philosophy of adventure education (Kraft, 1985; Sakofs, 1985). Freud, who developed a model based on the psychodynamic theory, suggests that thought and behavior are outcomes based on the emotional development of childhood (Cohen and Rae, 1987). According to Freud, healthy emotional development means balancing the desires of the id, the ego, and the superego. In achieving this balance one becomes more concerned with others, and less concerned with self. As a child we are more egoistic and become more altruistic as we move towards adulthood. As the superego develops, our level of maturity deepens, and we are able to focus more on the affairs of others. According to Kraft (1985), Freud's ideas have made an impact on adventure education. "Although most experiential educators would not see themselves as deterministic in their viewpoints as many Freudians, they nevertheless owe a debt for the insights gained about human behavior and motivation" (p. 21). Adventure educators have tapped into the field of psychology because they realize that their programs affect behavior and motivation. Organizations such as Healthcare International, Psychiatric Institutes of America, Charter Medical, and Hospital Corporations of America now offer specialized treatment in experiential therapy (Weider, 1990, p. 44). They primarily use high and low element ropes courses to help individuals develop skills concerning leadership capabilities, communication, cooperation, and trust. Individual goals are often predetermined before encountering the ropes course and then are later discussed in individual and group discussions. The experiential therapy industry continues to grow.

Another psychologist whose ideas might be of use to adventure education is Erikson. In *Childhood and Society* he outlines the "eight ages of man." The first of these eight stages through which one must advance in order to develop a healthy personality is that of trust. Erikson describes it as follows, "It is against this powerful combination of a sense of having been deprived, of having been divided, and of having been abandoned-that basic trust must maintain itself throughout life" (1950, p. 250). Developing trust is a key educational aim in adventure education for adolescents as well as adults. Activities such as belaying, trust falls, and trust hikes are used not only to develop trust in the younger ages, but to renew one's sense of trust with older individuals as well.

Trust is such an important issue in adventure education that program curricula often begin with a series of trust exercises which help individuals break down barriers so that they can begin working together as a group. These

exercises are often used as a metaphor for life. For example, the fourteen foot initiative wall requires that individuals be lifted high above the ground and pulled over the top of the wall. This task is difficult and scary and involves trusting the entire group. In life there are also difficult and scary tasks we must complete and having accomplished the fourteen foot wall helps us realize that trust and support from others makes these tasks easier to accomplish.

Goldstein (1939) a psychologist who worked with young children stated that, "In the innumerable repetitions of children, we are not dealing with the manifestation of a senseless drive for repetition, but with the tendency to completion and perfection... The nearer we are to perfection, the stronger is the need to perform. This is valid for children as well as adults..." (p. 196). These ideas led Goldstein towards developing a theory based on self actualization. He may be credited for creating the concept of self-actualization, but it was Abraham Maslow who picked up where Goldstein left off and brought us a clearer picture of this theory.

Adventure educators have begun to incorporate some of Maslow's ideas into their theory of education (Kraft, 1985,1991). In *Toward a Psychology of Being*, Maslow (1962) discusses several ideas concerning growth and self-actualization. One idea is that there are two forces which pull the individual in opposite directions. One force makes the individual "cling to safety and defensiveness out of fear, tending to regress backward, hanging on to the past...," and the other, "impels him forward toward wholeness of self and uniqueness of self, toward full functioning of all his capacities, toward confidence in the face of the external world at the same time that he can accept his deepest, real, unconscious self" (p. 44). The force which makes us cling to safety can at times deter us from growing.

In adventure education this force can easily be seen at work. For example, many individuals are afraid of the heights encountered in rock climbing or on ropes courses and these individuals tend to avoid such activities. If people can free themselves from this fear and overcome the challenge, they may discover new strengths. Growth takes place in new dimensions. The dichotomy between safety and risk coincides with the commonly held assumption, "people are more capable than they think they are." If we can free ourselves of this fear we can come closer to reaching our true potentials.

A second idea which stems from the self-actualization theory is that of personal growth. Maslow (1962) defined self-actualization as "an episode, or a spurt in which the powers of the person come together in a particularly efficient and intensely enjoyable way, and in which he is more integrated and less split, more open for experience, more idiosyncratic, more perfectly expressive or spontaneous, or fully functioning, more creative, more humorous, more ego-transcending, more independent of his lower needs, etc." (p.

91). This process, which is one of developing personal growth, is foundational to adventure education, and often times is the result of overcoming certain challenges or risks. Maslow (1962) supported the notion that challenge can be a catalyst for growth when he stated that: "We learn also about our own strengths and limits and extend them by overcoming difficulties, by straining ourselves to the utmost, by meeting challenge and hardship, even by failing" (p. 187).

Choice is another component of the self actualization theory. Maslow (1962) believed that all individuals, including children must learn to make their own decisions. When others constantly make decisions for children it does not allow them to develop judgement and their own personal standards. If meaningful growth is to take place individuals must have the freedom to choose their own direction of travel. In adventure education this opportunity is provided when individuals determine their own level of participation.

Another well known psychologist who took a humanistic approach to learning and developed certain ideas important to adventure education was Piaget (Sakofs, 1985; Kraft, 1991). Piaget's psychological schema on intellectual development consists of several stages of which formal operations is the last. During this stage, which takes place during adolescence, individuals develop the ability to reason in a complex fashion. Piaget drew his conclusions about this stage from a number of empirical tests which were somewhat similar, at least in theory, to the problem solving initiatives in adventure education. For example, with "the pendulum problem" students were supposed to figure out what factors, or combination of factors, caused the pendulum to oscillate the fastest (Ginsburg and Opper, 1969, p. (182). They were allowed to experiment and test out their ideas. From these tests Piaget realized that these children were able to make rational plans and carry them out in an orderly fashion, which led him to conclude that learning is a process of discovering, and that we learn best by exploring and experiencing our world.

The nature of human beings as seen by Piaget suggests that we are curious about things and are motivated to learn. We are eager to discover things about ourselves and the world we live in. Adventure education takes a similar view of human nature. Programs are designed to allow participants to discover more about their inner strengths. Adventure educators do not assume to know what is in the best interest of the student, and therefore, do not force individuals to participate. They assume that individuals have chosen to participate because they are motivated to learn. This view of human nature can be seen in several commonly used phrases such as, "learning by doing", "discover your inner strengths", and "discovery learning."

Finally, Rogers has added depth to adventure education's theory (Kraft, 1985). His book *Freedom to Learn* was very important to nontraditional approaches such as adventure education. "To free curiosity; to permit individuals to go charging off in new directions dictated by their own interests; to unleash the sense of inquiry; to open everything to questioning and exploration; to recognize that everything is in process of change-here is an experience I can never forget" (1969, p. 105). This statement suggests that in order for education to be truly meaningful teachers must allow their students the freedom to pursue questions and problems which are most meaningful to their own particular lives. When this happens students not only learn formal academic information, but they learn about themselves. There is an emotional investment because it is a real problem which has bearing upon their life.

This is exactly what takes place in adventure education. Participants learn technical information, but they also learn about themselves. For example, on a canoe trip individuals learn about the canoe, how to carry it, how to use different paddling strokes, and how to steer; but they are also learning about leadership, endurance, communication, and cooperation. They are faced with real problems on a day to day basis which affects their safety and comfort. The field of adventure education agrees with Rogers and is trying to educate the whole person which includes both intellectual and emotional development.

Current psychologists continue to develop and expand upon the theories and ideas mentioned above, but it was individuals such as Freud, Erikson, Goldstein, Maslow, Piaget, and Rogers whose work contributed most directly to adventure education. Their early psychological writings helped create and strengthen some of adventure education's foundational ideas. The construction, and ongoing reconstruction, of these ideas have helped develop and strengthen the philosophy of adventure education.

From Plato and Aristotle, to Dewey and Rogers, thinkers have examined how people grow mentally, physically, and morally. We have seen in this chapter that adventure education has clear foundational principles drawn from the long history of Western philosophical thought. Assertions containing these principles will be examined in chapters three, four, and five by using a method called the critical analysis.

# REFERENCES

Aristotle, *Nichomachean Ethics*. Martin Ostwald (Ed.). New York: Bobbs Merrill Co. Inc., 1962. Bambrough, R. *The Philosophy of Aristotle*. New York: The New American Library, 1963.

Cohen, S. and Rae, G. *Growing Up With Children*. New York: Holt, Rinehart, and Winston, 1987.

Crosby, A. A critical look: The philosophical foundations of experiential education. In R. Kraft and M. Sakofs (Eds.), *The Theory of Experiential Education*. Boulder: The Association for Experiential Education, 1985.

Dewey, J. *Democracy and Education*. New York: The Free Press, 1916.

Dewey J. *Experience and Education*. New York: MacMillan Publishing Co., 1938.

Erikson, E. *Childhood and Society*. New York: W.W. Norton and Co., 1950.

Ginsburg H. and Opper, S. *Piaget's Theory of Intellectual Development*. New Jersey: Prentice Hall, 1969.

Goldstein, K. *The Organism: A Holistic Approach to Biology Derived from Pathological Data in Man*. New York: American Book Co., 1939.

Hunt J. S. Ethics and experiential education as professional practice. *Journal of Experiential Education*. 1991. *14*, 2.

Hunt, J.S. Dewey's philosophical method and its influence on his philosophy of education. In R. Kraft and M. Sakofs (Eds.), *The Theory of Experiential Education*. Boulder: The Association for Experiential Education, 1985.

James, T. Sketch of a moving spirit: Kurt Hahn. In R. Kraft and M. Sakofs *The Theory of Experiential Education*. Boulder: Association for Experiential Education, 1985.

James, T. The paradox of safety and risk. *Journal of Experiential Education*. 1980, Fall, 20.

James, T. Kurt Hahn and the Aims of Education. *Journal of Experiential Education*. 1990, *13*, 1.

Kraft, R. J. Towards a theory of experiential learning. In R. Kraft and M. Sakofs (Eds.), *The Theory of Experiential Education*. Boulder: Association for Experiential Education, 1985.

Kraft, R.J. Experiential learning. In J. Miles And S. Priest (Eds.) *Adventure Education*. State College: Venture Publishing, 1990.

Maslow, A. *Toward a Psychology of Being*. New York: The Free Press, 1962.

Plato, *Plato's Republic*. G.M.A. Grube (Ed.), Indianapolis: Hackett Publishing Co., 1974.

Plato, *The Republic of Plato*. F.M. Cornford (Ed.), London: Oxford University Press, 1941.

Plato, *Theaetetus*. B. Jowett (Ed.), Indianapolis: The Bobbs Merrill Co., 1949.

Richards A. Kurt Hahn. In J. Miles and S. Priest (Eds.) *Adventure Education*. State College: Venture Publishing, 1990.

Rogers C. *Freedom to Learn*. Columbus: Charles E. Merrill Publishing, 1969.

Rousseau, J. J. *Emile or On Education*. A. Bloom (Ed.) New York: Basic Books, Inc. 1979.

Sakofs, M. Piaget-A psychological rationale for experiential education. In R. Kraft and M. Sakofs (Eds.), *The Theory of Experiential Education*. Boulder: Association for Experiential Education, 1985.

Skidelsky, R. *English Progressive Schools*. Baltimore: Penguin Books Inc. 1969.

Weider, R. Experiential therapy: An adventure in self discovery enters the psychiatric hospital. In J. Miles and S. Priest (Eds.) *Adventure Education*. State College: Venture Publishing Inc., 1990.

Whitehead, A. N. *Process and Reality- An Essay in Cosmology*. D.R. Griffin and D.W. Sherburne (Eds.) New York: The Free Press, 1929.

Wichmann, T.F. Babies and bath water: Two experiential heresies. In R. Kraft and M. Sakofs (Eds.), *The Theory of Experiential Education*. Boulder: The Association For Experiential Education, 1985.

# CONDUCTING A CRITICAL ANALYSIS

*For any theory and set of practices is dogmatic which
is not based upon critical examination of its own
underlying principles (Dewey, 1938, p. 22).*

According to Kneller, (1991) three modes or styles for conducting philosophy include speculative, prescriptive, and analytic. Speculative philosophy attempts to place meaning on the whole rather than the individual parts. It brings ideas together as opposed to breaking them down and tries to make sense of the big picture. "It is the attempt to find a coherence in the whole realm of thought and experience" (p. 147). Prescriptive philosophy places value on ideas and behavior. It tries to determine what is right or good, and then offers guidelines for appropriate actions. Analytic philosophy focuses on the meaning of ideas, words, and concepts. It attempts to "examine the assumptions and beliefs that lie behind educational decisions and practices" (VanScotter et.al, 1994, p. 67).

An analytic approach to philosophy, called critical analysis, will be discussed in this chapter. The primary focus of this chapter is to explain how to conduct a critical analysis, specifically for examining philosophies of education.

Critical analysis was developed by Apps (1985) for the primary purpose of examining a field's assumptions about theory and practice. It can also be used as a tool to help educators become more aware of their philosophies of education, and to point out discrepancies between what they say in theory and what they actually do in practice.

Brookfield (1987) is also a strong advocate of critical analysis methodology. He argues that this approach is effective because it helps educators recognize when they are using false assumptions. He also suggests that assumptions must be challenged in order to bring about important change.

The critical analysis consists of two important ideas: identifying assumptions and raising questions that challenge these assumptions. Apps (1985) suggests that the first step in the process is to identify assumptions, however in order to accomplish this, one must first identify assertions from which assumptions may be drawn. The critical analysis methodology that will be used in this book varies somewhat from Apps's, and will consist of three steps.

The first step is to identify assertions that reflect adventure education's philosophy. The second entails drawing out explicit and implicit assumptions, and the third is to raise questions that may point out discrepancies between theory and practice.

Three assertions from a Hurricane Island Outward Bound brochure will be used as examples to explain why they reflect this organization's philosophy of education.

**Assertion One:** *Our classroom is the wilderness and our teachings are based on experience* (Hurricane Island Outward Bound Course Catalog, 1996, p. 6), asserts that experience is a primary teaching tool, and therefore reflects Outward Bound's views on learning. Teaching and learning fall under the branch of philosophy known as epistemology which is the study of how we gain knowledge. It attempts to answer questions such as, what is the source of knowledge, is there more than one way to gain knowledge, and how do we know when we have acquired it?

**Assertion Two:** *The value of the course comes from finding the strength to move beyond difficulties to discover new potential within yourself* (1996, p. 6), implies that it is of our nature to find strength in the midst of difficult challenges, and is therefore a reflection on human nature. Human nature falls under the branch of philosophy known as metaphysics which studies the nature of reality. Metaphysics attempts to answer questions about the way things really are in the world such as, is the world moving towards steady state or is it in constant flux, is risk real or only a matter of perception, and do people have free will or is life predetermined? Many of the questions about human nature have opposing ideas. For instance, is it of our nature to be good or evil, lazy or motivated, free or controlled by external stimuli?

**Assertion Three:** *Hurricane Island Outward Bound School helps students develop self esteem, self reliance, and concern for others and our environment through rigorous outdoor programs* (1996, p. 6), suggests that Outward Bound teaches people about moral behavior, and therefore is a reflection on their views of morality. Morality falls under the branch of philosophy known as ethics.

Ethics examines questions about right and wrong and tries to determine what actions ought to be taken. It attempts to answer questions about how we should treat one another, the earth, and living creatures. It also studies theories about how we should determine our actions.

Epistemology, metaphysics, and ethics are three important components that help define a philosophy of education. Drawing out assumptions pertaining to these three components can help educators become aware of their beliefs about teaching and learning, their views of the learner, and the educational values they hold. Taken together they are what constitute a philosophy of education.

The second step in the critical analysis methodology is to draw out explicit and implicit assumptions. The following is a list of four assumptions drawn from assertion one: *Our classroom is the wilderness and our teachings are based on experience.*

1. Wilderness is the primary classroom.
2. Experience is a critical component of the learning process on Outward Bound courses.
3. Without direct experience learning is less apt to occur.
4. Outward Bound instructors never use indoor classrooms for teaching.

The first two assumptions are explicit because they have basically the same meaning as the assertion. Assumptions three and four are implicit because they are not plainly apparent or directly expressed in the assertion. Explicit assumptions are more obvious because they are drawn directly from verbal or written statements, but implicit assumptions may be hidden and require looking beyond the statement itself. Implicit assumptions are often overlooked, but are extremely valuable because they can help point out inconsistencies between theory and practice.

For instance, Outward Bound states that *the wilderness is its classroom*, which implies it does not use indoor classrooms. This implicit assumption however, does not hold true. Outward Bound instructors often use indoor rooms with tables, chairs, and chalkboards for teaching and demonstration purposes.

The third and last step is to raise questions about the assumptions. Here are several questions raised from the four assumptions above.

1. Is wilderness the best classroom?
2. Are some content areas better taught indoors?
3. How important is physical comfort when teaching or learning?
4. What is the difference between direct and indirect experience?

5.  Does indirect experience have any educational value?

6.  Does Outward Bound ever use indirect experience in their teachings?

Such questions are important in helping a program identify potential pitfalls with theory and practice. They may help a program refine and improve their teaching strategies and techniques, and are the catalyst to change.

The critical analysis methodology can also be used to help educators become more aware of their own personal philosophies of education. To illustrate I will explain how I have used it to analyze my own philosophy and teaching practices. I am a University professor and teach several theory based courses. In one of my semester long courses, I taught students how to conduct a critical analysis and then asked them to use the methodology on myself. I mentioned that they could use any written material such as the syllabus, as well as any verbal statements I made in class that may reflect my personal philosophy of education. Part way through the semester I did a verbal evaluation where students had the opportunity to discuss their critical analyses of my teaching. One student identified this assertion that I made early in the course when I first explained my personal philosophy of education.

*I believe strongly in experiential learning where students take an active role in the learning process; and in order for learning to be effective students must apply what they are learning.*

One assumption he drew from this assertion was, college students must have opportunities to apply theory outside the classroom during the scheduled class period. He then raised this question, "if experiential learning is so important to you, then why are there only four class periods out of 16 where we are actually out of the classroom facilitating activities with elementary school groups?" This question prompted me to rethink my definition of experiential learning. I use a variety of techniques in the classroom, such as individual and group presentations, group projects, and debates to motivate and engage students in their learning. While these techniques may promote critical thinking, they do not provide direct experience. I now try to incorporate more direct experience outside the classroom that provides opportunities for college students to do programming with different groups.

Another student identified this assertion.

*Individual presentations are one way to engage the learner in critical thinking.*

Here is one assumption that was identified: when people are talking they are engaged in critical thinking. The follow up question was, "are students engaged in critical thinking every time they do presentations?" The use of individual presentations is a classroom technique that forces students to talk about reading assignments. A number of students are selected on days when readings are assigned, to give a two or three minute presentation that allows them to express their ideas on the material. The original format was open ended so some students chose to take issue with the material and raise thought provoking questions, while others chose to outline the main points. Presenting an outline on a reading requires less thinking because students can simply reiterate the main points, without understanding or analyzing the ideas contained in the reading.

This student's critical analysis led me to change the format of individual presentations. I now have students take issue with the material which encourages them to analyze what they are reading. I also ask presenters to explain how the ideas and theories can be applied in real life settings. This change has been significant. Students are now reading their assignments with a critical eye, and are much more engaged in class discussions. This simple change, has ultimately created more excitement in the classroom.

A third student identified this assertion, which once again was made early in the semester at the beginning of the course.

*In this course we are going to read articles that discuss adventure programs that cater to a variety of different populations including adjudicated youth, school groups, corporate, and women.*

One assumption the student drew from this assertion was, adjudicated youth, education, corporate, and women are the most common groups to work with in the field of adventure education. Her question was, "aren't there other groups that use adventure activities for programming such as physically disabled and other psychiatric patients?" My reality was different from the woman that raised this question. I chose those articles because I have previous experience working with these different populations. I was not comfortable talking about something I had no experience with, but she was correct in suggesting that these other populations should be considered. This led me to expand my course curriculum to include articles about these other populations. I also solicit help to teach this section of the course, from students that have had prior experience working with these groups.

The critical analysis has helped me strengthen my philosophy of education by broadening my views on learning. Before the analysis I thought that if I could get students to talk during class discussions, then experiential learning was occurring. My definition has expanded, and now I try to provide more learning opportunities outside the classroom that have real and immediate consequences for students. No doubt the process of experiential learning should include discussions, but it should also provide opportunities to apply theory in real life settings.

The analysis helped me broaden my views on the learner. Early in the semester students seemed apathetic and resistant to learning. When introduced to the critical analysis they realized that it could truly change course content and structure, and therefore, became very serious about learning how to use this methodology. This indicated a concern for receiving a quality education. Most students are motivated to learn, especially when they are given the freedom to determine how to make course material more relevant to their lives.

This analysis expanded my view of reality. Teachers are shaped largely by their past experiences, which to an extent, determines what they teach and how they teach. I was accustomed to operating from my own reality and past experiences, but this analysis made me realize that if the course material or teaching methodology is not interesting to students, then a change must be made so that learning is more apt to occur.

Finally, the analysis created a positive change in the classroom environment. Students were excited to share their analyses with the class, and seemed more willing to express their true feelings about the class after doing the analysis. One reason for this may be because they were using a method that allowed them to analyze statements and actions on an intellectual level, rather than an emotional level. They were following a three step methodology which objictified the process and removed them from personal attacks on the teacher.

When I first thought of having my class conduct a critical analysis on my teaching I was a little hesitant because it could point out some problems with my teaching that might require me to do more work. I had become familiar with certain materials and methodologies, and was slowly becoming resistant to change. I was also concerned that my University colleagues might feel that I was giving my students too much freedom in determining the direction of the course content and teaching methodologies used. In reality however, it was one the best things I have ever done as a teacher. Without their feedback I would still be teaching the same way.

How can teachers implement this process into their classrooms? One class period (50-60 minutes) usually provides enough time to teach students how to conduct a critical analysis. For instance, I begin with a brief explanation (five minutes) of the methodology, and provide an example which I place on an overhead that includes one assertion, four assumptions, and six questions. The overhead is reproduced in Figure 2.1. I then have students break into small groups (two or three), and have them practice conducting their own analyses by identifying one assertion, three or four assumptions, and several questions. I provide 10-15 minutes for them to conduct their analyses, and then have them present their analyses to the class. The overhead is left on so they can refer back to the example if necessary. It is also helpful, before they begin, to clarify differences between assertions, and explicit and implicit assumptions, which will enhance accuracy when conducting their analyses. Once students have learned how to conduct an analysis, I explain that they will be using this methodology periodically throughout the semester to examine my teaching practices. Two class periods, one at the midpoint and the other at the end of the semester are set aside for students to discuss their critical analyses of my teaching. These are verbal evaluations which are done by sitting in a circle, and one by one, students read their critical analyses to the group while the teacher takes notes.

The critical analysis has numerous applications, and can be used to examine written statements found in books, articles, policy and procedure manuals, advertising brochures, mission statements; as well as verbal statements made by educators. In the next three chapters, the critical analysis is used to examine the philosophy of adventure education. Brochures from programs such as Outward Bound, National Outdoor Leadership School (NOLS), Project Adventure, and Nantahala Outdoor Center will be examined. Assertions that reflect adventure education's views on learning, risk and human nature, and aims of education will be identified and analyzed. It is my intention that instructors will also use the critical analysis as a tool to examine their own personal philosophies of education. It behooves educators to identify and analyze their own underlying assumptions about teaching and learning so they can refine and enhance their practices.

---

**ASSERTION**

Our classroom is the wilderness and our teachings are based on direct experience (Hurricane Island Outward Bound Brochure, 1996).

**ASSUMPTIONS**

1.  Wilderness is the primary classroom.
2.  Experience is a critical component of the learning process on outward bound courses.
3.  Without direct experience learning is less apt to occur.
4.  Outward bound instructors never use indoor classrooms for teaching.

**Questions**

1. Is wilderness the best classroom?
2. Are some content areas better taught indoors?
3. How important is physical comfort when teaching and learning?
4. What is the difference between direct and indirect experience?
5. Does indirect experience have any educational value?

---

**Figure 2.1:**    *An example of the critical analysis methodology.*

# REFERENCES

Apps, J. W. *Improving Practice in Continuing Education*. San Francisco: Jossey-Bass Publishers, 1985.

Brookfield, S. D. *Developing Critical Thinkers: Challenging Adults to Explore Alternative Ways of Thinking and Acting*. San Francisco: Jossey Bass Publishers, 1987.

Dewey, J. *Experience and Education*. New York: Macmillan Publishing Company, 1938.

Hurricane Island Outward Bound catalog, Rockland, Maine, 1996.

Kneller, G. F. The relevance of philosophy. In J. Johnson, et. al. (Eds.) *Reflections on American Education: Classic and Contemporary Readings*. Boston: Allyn and Bacon, 1991.

VanScotter, R. D., Haas, J. D., Kraft, R. K., and Schott, J. D. *Social Foundations of Education*. Englewood Cliffs: Prentice Hall, Inc., 1991.

# VIEWS ON THE LEARNING PROCESS

*What we want and need is education pure and
simple, and we shall make surer and faster
progress when we devote ourselves to finding out
just what education is and what conditions have
to be satisfied in order that education may be a
reality and not a name or a slogan (Dewey,
1938, p. 90, 91).*

In 1938 Dewey wrote an influential book titled *Experience and
Education*. In it he argues for an educational process that includes
both theory and practice. He also argues that the prefixes placed in
front of the term "education" can actually inhibit our thinking. Progressive and traditional education were two opposing camps that Dewey
tried to synthesize. He suggests that by taking positive aspects from
each, leads to a more effective philosophy of education.

Today the field of adventure education continues to struggle with this
same problem. Adventure educators lay claims to the experiential learning process, yet often fail to realize the importance of traditional methodologies. This chapter will examine different learning processes for the
purpose of broadening the understanding of how they are used in adventure education.

> **ASSERTION:** "Traditional education is theory rich and practice poor." (Rogers Memorial Hospital Ropes Course brochure, 1990, p. 1)
>
> **ASSUMPTION ONE:** Adventure education is different than traditional education.

One difference between traditional and adventure education, at least in theory, is the learning process used. Classroom learning, which is usually affiliated with traditional education, begins with theory and ends with practice; whereas experiential learning, the process most often associated with adventure education, begins with experience and ends with theory.

*Classroom learning usually begins with the dispensing of a particular body of information (via book, film, or lecture). This information is then meant to be organized and assimilated by the student and finally 'learned' when it is actually applied through action. Experiential learning takes just the reverse track. The learner is presented with the opportunity to carry out an action and see the effects of that action. From this base, general concepts and principles are generated" (Gager, 1982, p. 31).*

This implies that the way in which an individual comes to know the subject matter is different as well. With classroom learning retention is the goal, which suggests that in order to learn we must first have information presented to us and then memorize it for later use. With experiential learning, on the other hand, we must first do something with the subject matter which then generates ideas. Both formats include thinking, but of different kinds. Memorizing information for later use is the type of thinking elicited with traditional education, whereas planning and testing ideas is the type of thinking required of experiential learning.

In reality however, adventure educators use the traditional approach all the time. They have no choice but to use this process because students must first understand certain information, such as safety procedures, before they can participate in the activity. For instance, when teaching rock climbing, instructors do not allow students to experience it first and then generate ideas, they explain equipment use, belay procedures, and safety precautions, and then allow students to apply this theory by actually climbing some rock.

This suggests that adventure education may be based as much on the principles of traditional as they are on experiential education. The reasons why the traditional approach is so effective in adventure education is because students immediately apply what they hear. During belay school, for example, instructors explain and demonstrate the technique and then students apply this theory directly following instruction.

**ASSUMPTION TWO:** Traditional education lacks a practical component?

This is not necessarily true. According to Coleman (1976) in, "Differences Between Experiential and Classroom Learning," there are four steps in the traditional information assimilation learning process. The first three steps are theoretical where students listen and retain information but the last step entails, "moving from the cognitive and symbolic-processing sphere to the sphere of action" (p. 51). This is where information, through application, becomes knowledge.

Labs, field trips, cooperative education programs, and extracurricular activities such as student government and student newspapers all offer students the opportunity to apply information from the classroom. Students can perform experiments in science labs, take nature hikes and learn about plants and animals, and study business by actually taking a job or internship. Such opportunities provide practical hands-on learning.

This suggests, at least with certain courses, that traditional education contains a practical component, and therefore, has the potential to be just as complete as the experiential learning process. Unfortunately, the traditional approach may not be as effective in formal classroom settings because the process often does not reach the last step which is application. Little (1981) argues that college students may learn theory and are able to retain large amounts of information but in many cases are unable to apply it once they enter the work force. Furthermore, he mentions this as a primary criticism of employers because it is, "obviously a case of incomplete learning" (p. 10).

We live in a society that continues to accumulate more information, and in turn places a responsibility on the schools to disseminate it. Teachers have a limited amount of class time in which to cover required information. Therefore they feel forced to employ what's commonly perceived as the most time efficient method. This often means lecturing.

Students, especially in higher education, are also on a tight schedule. Increases in tuition force them to take more credits and finish earlier, leaving little time for much beyond memorization. Application of information is put on hold until graduation, by which time information may be forgotten or lost. This learning environment is inadequate because it is steeped in theory and lacking in practice. We are efficient at getting information out to students, but inefficient at providing them with meaningful learning experiences. Dewey (1916) was probably one of the earliest educators to state this idea. He argues for students to be placed in situations that are similar to those outside the school. Such situations are likely to be more relevant, which will arouse interest and engage students in the experience. "To realize what an experience, or empirical situation, means, we have to call to mind the sort of situation that presents itself outside of school; the sort of occupations that interest and engage activity in ordinary life" (p. 154).

In this statement Dewey was responding to an educational system that did not provide students with meaningful learning experiences because it relied on extrinsic motivation. When students are presented with information that is primarily of the teacher's interest, they have to be motivated by external controls such as tests and grades. Dewey argues that this process has little connection to the student's lives, and therefore contains few intrinsic learning incentives.

To ensure that meaningful learning occurs, educators using traditional methods need to provide opportunities and time for the last step which is practical application. Typically, this is easy for adventure educators because students are participating in activities immediately after receiving necessary information.

**ASSUMPTION THREE:** Experiential learning is more effective than traditional methods.

If what differentiates experiential learning from classroom learning is the inclusion of a problem or challenge, then this assumption may hold true. Coleman (1976) argues that when experience comes at the beginning of the cycle one is motivated to continue through the steps until an answer is discovered. But, this is true only if the experience presents a

Photograph courtesy of John McDonald

challenge or problem to the student. This suggests that when a problem, which has direct relevancy is presented, students become emotionally engaged in the learning process.

For example, bushwhacking with a map and compass is an experience which has a desired outcome. The experience motivates students to learn how to use the map and compass because they need this knowledge in order to reach their destination. This experience directly affects their lives because if they get lost they may have to spend the night in the woods without food or sleeping bags.

Coleman (1976) also suggests that this process enhances one's retention: "A final property of experiential learning is that it appears to be less easily forgotten than learning through information assimilation" (p. 58). Dewey (1916) also alludes to this notion:

*Before the child goes to school, he learns with his hand, eye, and ear, because they are organs of the process of doing something from which meaning results. The boy flying a kite has to keep his eye on the kite, and has to note the various pressures of the string on his hand. His senses are avenues of knowledge not because external facts are somehow "conveyed" to the brain, but because they are used in doing something with a purpose (p. 142).*

The use of our senses is crucial to the experiential learning process, because, when we are directly involved in an experience, all of our senses are engaged. For example, when we sit in a classroom and listen to someone read a story about a climbing trip, all of our senses are not as engaged as when we are actually out climbing.

These benefits suggest that the experiential learning process is more meaningful than traditional methods because it motivates students and helps them remember. However, the process is not without its faults. According to Coleman (1976): "The weakest link in the experiential process of learning appears to lie in the third step, in generalizing from particular experiences to a general principle applicable in other circumstances..."( p. 58). This alludes to the importance of debriefing or discussion at the end of participation in adventure activities so that students can make connections between present and future experiences. When instructors lack theoretical sophistication, important learning may be lost. Because students are not always able to make connections between a specific experience and its relationship to life in general, adventure educators should understand the theory of experiential learning and allot time for reflection and discussion at the conclusion of each activity. For example, good ropes course instructors should be able to explain the experiential learning process, and demonstrate how it is being utilized on the course. They should understand why both action and reflection are necessary, show how theory and practice are bound together, and explain how this process might apply to other areas of life such as home, school, work activities, and interpersonal relationships.

When learning lacks a theoretical connection between the experience, and how that experience might be applied to other similar experiences, learning may go awry. Likewise, when students are given theoretical concepts without the opportunity to apply them, the learning process does not reach completion. These situations lead to frustration and lower one's level of motivation. Therefore, adventure educators should work towards incorporating both theory and practice into their learning environments. Dewey (1938) sums this idea up as follows:

> *I do not wish to close, however, without recording my firm belief that the fundamental issue is not of new versus old education nor of progressive against traditional education but a question of what anything whatever must be to be worthy of the name education (p. 90).*

**ASSERTION:** "Our course designs are based on the principles of experiential education..." (Kurt Hahn Leadership Center brochure, 1991, p. 1).

**ASSUMPTION:** Experiential education is the same thing as adventure education.

Individuals confuse these two terms from reading statements like the one above, but there is also confusion due to the fact that the Association for Experiential Education (AEE) contains a large constituency of adventure educators. AEE hosts several regional conferences and one International conference each year, and since there are numerous adventure programs affiliated with this association, it is not unusual to see many themes and topics at these conferences revolving around adventure education. Some people who attend these conferences may leave with the impression that adventure education is the same thing as experiential education.

But experiential education is much broader in application, and is often viewed as a learning process rather than a content. A hands-on approach is often used with this educational process, but it is not always necessary. What is necessary is that people problem solve by developing a plan, and then test out this plan in reality. Dewey (1916) refers to this process as the reflective experience which includes perplexity, surveying the information at hand, formulating a hypothesis, and testing this plan against reality (p. 150).

This learning process can be utilized in teaching many subjects, including more formal curricula such as math, biology, chemistry, and physics. For example, a math teacher who uses survey instruments to teach the class how to calculate the number of board feet in a tree is using an experiential approach to learning. Similarly when students collect water samples to test pollution levels, or mix chemicals to produce certain reactions, they are learning experientially. The goal is to learn principles and methods of math or chemistry, but to do so they engage in problem-solving that requires hands-on involvement.

Adventure educators also use this learning process while teaching a variety of activities such as rock climbing, canoeing, and map and compass work. People test out their ideas when they try certain moves to climb difficult sections on the rock, use certain strokes to keep the canoe going straight, or navigate unfamiliar ground using a map and compass. But adventure education is different than experiential education in that it has a specific content area which revolves around a variety of adventure activities. People who participate in adventure education learn skills such as knot tying, belaying, and climbing, yet even though the content entails learning specific skills, the purpose is to help people learn more about themselves and the world they live in. Educational benefits include such things as enhanced self esteem, stronger leadership skills, greater willingness to take risks, and renewed self confidence. Unlike experiential education, it is a field that has a specific content area and well-defined educational goals.

Even though experiential education and adventure education are distinctly different from one another, there is overlap in that adventure education utilizes experience in its learning process. Adventure educators often refer to themselves as experiential educators because they are using a hands-on approach to education, but just because people are doing something with their hands doesn't necessarily mean that learning is taking place. The term is being properly used as long as adventure educators are engaging their students in the reflective experience, and improperly used if they are providing experiences which do not require any problem solving and reflection.

> **ASSERTION:** "The course is education in action: students learn by doing, not just watching or reading about it" (National Outdoor Leadership School Brochure, 1993, p. 12).
>
> **ASSUMPTION ONE:** When we do something we learn something.

According to Dewey (1916) learning requires more than just "doing".

*One may learn by doing something which he does not understand; even in the most intelligent action, we do much which we do not mean, because the largest portion of the connections of the act we consciously intend are not perceived or anticipated. But we learn only because after the act is performed we note results which we had not noted before (p. 78).*

For Dewey, one of the conditions of learning is that we make a connection between what we do and the consequences which result. For example someone, by chance, could physically manipulate a climbing rope so that the end result is a bowline on a bight, but if the individual can't duplicate it, and does not understand that what has been tied is a bowline on a bight, then learning has not occurred.

Furthermore, Dewey (1916) suggests that once we learn something by doing, we are also able to make connections between one learning experience and the next. He suggests that when our actions become automatic it may increase our level of skill, but if it does not lead to new insights or connections, then it limits rather than widens our learning horizon (p. 78). For example, after learning how to tie the bowline on a bight the individual should then be able to use this knot for diverse situations found in rock climbing and sailing. If there is no connection between one experience and the next, then learning is compartmentalized and its value is limited. The activity becomes merely an end in itself, rather than a means to enhance future learning.

ASSUMPTION TWO: Our bodies have to be physically involved in the learning process in order for adventure education to be effective.

For Dewey (1916), learning through experience does not have to include any physical involvement. In chapter five of *Democracy and Education* he states that, "The initial stage of that developing experience which is called thinking is experience" (p. 153). This suggests that learning via experience does not have to include any physical activity. Simply sitting with your eyes closed and thinking your way through a math problem can constitute an educative experience. For Dewey, it is important to note that the process of thinking is the same thing as learning through experience, and does not have to include any physical activity. Therefore, the process of thinking is an experience in and of itself.

His emphasis on thinking suggests that mind is the primary tool used in the learning process. In contrast, adventure education tends to emphasize the body, viewing physical involvement as necessary to complete the learning process. But, while activities are useful, they are not absolutely necessary. According to Dewey, physical involvement is neither a necessary or sufficient condition for learning.

There are numerous adventure-based programs which claim to offer experiential learning, yet in their brochures the concept is nothing more than a list of activities. Many programs often include all day participation in varied and numerous activities such as initiative games, ropes courses, rock climbing, and canoeing without any time left for discussion and reflection. People engage in these activities because they require physical participation. It is difficult to learn how to canoe without canoeing or climb without climbing, but when time for reflection is left out of this process, learning becomes secondary to the activity itself.

In summary, adventure education's views on the learning process place a strong emphasis on hands-on experience and physical activity. This is acceptable as long as it remembers the other half of the equation, which is reflection and the making of connections between what was done and why. This field is excellent at providing experiences for others, but if individual participants cannot make sense out of their experiences, or connect them to other experiences, this learning process is useless. Dewey (1938) sums up the danger by noting that, "a given experience may increase a person's automatic skill in a particular direction and yet tend to land him in a groove or rut" (p. 26). Therefore, when "doing" becomes overemphasized, adventure education's learning becomes lopsided and its activities become a series of unconnected experiences, each leading to its own dead end.

Photograph courtesy of John McDonald

To avoid the problem of becoming experience rich and theory poor, adventure educators must understand the concepts behind the learning process so that they can help people connect their experiences with everyday life. They must understand that impelling people into problem solving experiences engenders interest and motivation which is crucial if self-directed learning is to take place. Finally, on a broader scale, practitioners of adventure education should examine questions such as: what makes teaching and learning effective, why is experience so crucial to the learning process, and what are the implications and applications of adventure education? Addressing such questions requires that theoretical principles be explored, challenged, and expanded. Adventure educators can avoid the pitfalls of becoming experience rich by taking the initiative to continue their own learning which can lead to a fuller understanding of both the theory and practice in this field.

## DISCUSSION QUESTIONS

- Explain the differences and similarities between classroom learning and experiential learning.
- Explain why classroom learning and experiential learning may be equally effective?
- Under what circumstances should one use classroom learning over experiential learning?
- What is an advantage of using experiential learning over classroom learning?
- Explain the difference between experiential education and adventure education.
- What makes adventure education unique from other disciplines?
- What are some confusing issues about adventure education and experiential education?
- What are the essential components of the learning process?
- Why is the process of thinking an experience?

## REFERENCES

Coleman, J. in Keeton, M.T. (Ed) *Experiential Learning*. San Francisco: Jossey-Bass, 1976.

Dewey, J. *Democracy and Education*.New York: The Free Press, 1916.

Dewey J. *Experience and Education*. New York: MacMillan Publishing Co., 1938.

Gager, R. Experiential education: strengthening the learning process. *Child and Youth Services*. 1982, 4, 31-39.

Kurt Hahn Leadership Center Brochure, Morganton: North Carolina Outward Bound School, 1991.

Little, T. History and rationale for experiential learning. *National Society for Internships and Experiential Education*. 1981, 1-13

National Outdoor Leadership School Brochure, Lander, Wyoming, 1993

Rogers Memorial Hospital Ropes and Challenge course brochure, Oconomowoc, Wisconsin, 1991.

The Association for Experiential Education conference brochure, 1990.

# VIEWS ON RISK AND HUMAN NATURE

*"You emphasize safety in a high risk operation.
You emphasize safety but you don't kill the risk.
You emphasize safety as a rational man's effort at
survival, but we're going to go right ahead and
stick our head in the noose...that's the game"*
*(Unsoeld, 1977).*

Unsoeld's statement suggests that risk is crucial to any adventure experience. Facing the physical challenge of activities such as kayaking or mountaineering gets our adrenaline flowing and may even cause us, for an instant, to look death in the face. Risk is used to foster intellectual, physical, and spiritual growth, and is the element that distinguishes adventure education from other educational fields.

His statement also contains in it hidden assumptions about human nature. For instance, it implies that we avoid risk, but it is important to engage in such activities if we are going to learn and grow. The purpose of this chapter is to examine similar statements that contain assumptions about risk and human nature.

> **ASSERTION:** "The purpose of Outward Bound, simply expressed, is to foster personal growth" (Hurricane Island Outward Bound brochure, 1991, p. 1).
>
> **ASSUMPTION ONE:** Adventure education knows what it means by personal growth.

What does adventure education mean by personal growth? Does it mean technical growth, intellectual growth, psychological growth, all of the above, or something else entirely? Certainly, different programs have different emphases. For instance, some focus on adventure education skills and stress technical proficiency. Other programs may use adventure activities as a way to discuss philosophical underpinnings of adventure education. Still other programs use adventure education to help people with psychological issues; they are primarily concerned with building trust, confidence, and self-esteem, and are often therapeutic in application.

Whatever the program's emphasis, all adventure experiences have the potential to affect both the intellect and the emotions. When students negotiate the spider web, they must figure out a plan, communicate to one another, execute the plan, and risk being lifted in the air by other participants who might be total strangers. Accomplishing such tasks might require several attempts, and possibly rethinking old strategies in order to develop new ways of executing the plan. This is a thought-provoking process that may require various problem-solving strategies.

The adventure experience can also challenge the participants emotionally, requiring people to trust others to hold them up and not drop them to the ground. Overcoming such fears and accomplishing such tasks has the potential to raise confidence and self-esteem. Therefore, adventure education's definition of personal growth appears to include technical, emotional, and intellectual development.

ASSUMPTION TWO:   Risk is an essential element to the growth process.

J. Unsoeld (1985) in a keynote speech given for the Association for Experiential Education quoted W. Unsoeld as follows:

*We used to tell them in Outward Bound, when a parent would come and ask us, "Can you guarantee the safety of our son, Johnny?" And we finally decided to meet it head-on. We would say, No, we certainly can't Ma'am. We guarantee you the genuine chance of his death. And if we could guarantee his safety, the program would not be worth running. We do make one guarantee, as one parent to another. If you succeed in protecting your boy, as you are doing now, and as it's your motherly duty to do, you know, we applaud your watch dog tenacity. You should be protecting him. But, if you succeed, we guarantee you the death of his soul! (1985, p. 112)*

Unsoeld's point is well taken, especially in the field of adventure education. When risk is eliminated from adventure education some growth is eliminated as well. The force and impact would be very limited if there were no risk involved in the process. Yet, will one's soul die if not exposed to adventurous risk-taking situations? It is not clear what Unsoeld means by "death of his soul" but it is certainly not necessary to take an Outward Bound course in order to grow and develop into a healthy individual. For instance, teaching in a traditional classroom setting can also be an adventure which leads to personal growth. Rogers (1969) states that," it is only by risking himself in these new ways that the teacher can discover, for himself, whether or not they are effective, whether or not they are for him" (p. 115). Rogers argues that there is risk involved in teaching, and that in order for educators to grow they must take risks with their teaching methodologies. This concept is true of all occupations. If we want to grow and become better teachers, therapists, administrators, etc. then we must take risks.

Both Rogers and Unsoeld argue that risk is a necessary condition of growth. Taking a risk requires experimentation and trying new ideas, which in turn allows people an opportunity to step outside their preconceived boundaries and comfort levels. The amount of risk participants are able to handle will vary from person to person, but in order to grow they must be encountered. Some ideas might not work once they are put to practice, but if risks are not taken, current levels of knowledge cannot be expanded. Therefore, risk is a crucial ingredient to the growth process.

**ASSUMPTION THREE:**  Adventure education programs provide true risk-taking experiences that promote personal growth.

Are adventure education programs providing appropriate risk-taking experiences that lend themselves to both intellectual and emotional development? Not necessarily. On one hand, ropes course programs that herd their students through a high ropes course, element by element, with instructors who buckle their sit harnesses for them, tie their knots, lock their carabiners, and belay them are limiting the amount of responsibility for learning taking place. They are not consciously teaching their students any technical information that is important if students are to become more knowledgeable about the theory and practice of adventure education.

On the other hand, individuals can still be challenged even when their involvement with knot tying and belaying is eliminated. The element of risk is very real for most ropes course participants; therefore simply negotiating the activity itself will help students learn more about courage, self esteem, and trust. Some would argue that students have enough on their minds without having to worry about all the logistics of knot tying and belaying.

It is important to eliminate the possibility of student error, but it is also important to give people an opportunity to grow. This interplay between risk and growth has been discussed by numerous adventure educators. James (1980) states that, "Many are anxious that this form of education will lose its excitement and cease to be a powerful learning experience if it is made so safe that it lacks the spontaneity, the stress, the hard-earned achievements of a genuine adventure" (p. 20). No doubt this is a paradoxical situation that demands careful attention, but if the field of adventure education wants to optimize growth then learning should be taking place on both an intellectual and emotional level.

Most students are emotionally challenged by adventure activities, but they won't be intellectually challenged if the instructors do all the work for them. Hunt (1990) argues that "a program which has eliminated all student responsibility for safety and, therefore, all risk from its safety system is not really an adventure education program but is, rather, an amusement park" (p. 22). If growth includes enhancing self esteem, as well as learning technical skills, then adventure educators should allow students to participate in more than just the activity itself. They should allow them an opportunity to learn safety procedures, knot tying, and belaying, as well as participate in the activity.

In some ways it appears that the field of adventure education is schizophrenic. On one hand the theory is filled with statements that appeal to the rugged individual. Phrases such as "conquer yourself," "take the challenge," and "be a leader" imply that we should take risks which entail adventure and excitement, so that we can grow and become better people. Yet, student involvement, especially on ropes courses, is often limited to participating in the activity without learning any information concerning equipment and procedures. If adventure education's definition of personal growth includes both intellectual and emotional development then programs should allow students an opportunity to grow on more than just one level.

Photograph courtesy of John McDonald

> **ASSERTION:** "While there are dangers associated with the wilderness, our operating procedures insure that the risks you face are more perceived than real" (Outward Bound Revised Course Schedule brochure, 1991, p. 4).
>
> **ASSUMPTION ONE:** Adventure programs can control risk.

According to Hunt (1990), objective risk is a part of reality and it cannot be controlled. Objective risk refers to things beyond our control such as a rock fall, a lightning strike, or equipment failure. Such incidents are commonly referred to as freak accidents or acts of God, and the only way to avoid such risk is to avoid participating in adventure education activities altogether.

Freire (1970) agrees. In *Pedagogy of the Oppressed* he argues that education is a dynamic process which takes place in a reality that is continually transforming itself: "In problem-posing education, men develop their power to perceive critically the way they exist in the world with which and in which they find themselves; they come to see the world not as a static reality, but as a reality in process, in transformation" (p. 71).

If reality is in a continual state of flux, then some risks are certainly beyond our control. We can decide whether to stand under a tree or out in the open during a thunderstorm, but we cannot control how long the storm will last or where the lightning will strike. In this situation most us would not stand under a tree because statistics show that lightning will strike a taller object more often than open ground. This, however, does not guarantee that we won't be hit. We can take precautions but freak accidents do happen.

Dewey (1916) suggests that even thinking involves a risk. "Certainty cannot be guaranteed in advance," he writes. "The invasion of the unknown is of the nature of an adventure; we cannot be sure in advance" (p. 148). Of course, the act of thinking is not as dangerous as participating in an adventure activity, but the point here is that there are certain unknowns inherent in reality, and whether we are physically involved in an activity, or thinking about the possible actions we might take, we can never be absolutely certain of the future. Therefore, even

though adventure educators can control certain variables, such as equipment, navigation procedures, and safety techniques, risk is inherent in life and finally unavoidable.

> **ASSUMPTION TWO:**  The risk encountered in adventure education
> is only a matter of perception.

Hale (1985), director of the National Safety Network, describes adventure education as a business which focuses on involving people in activities where they encounter the risk of injury (p. 16). This suggests that risk in adventure education is not just a matter of perception, it is real. It is not just perceived, because people are put in situations where they really could get hurt, or even die.

Furthermore, even if the risk was more perceived than real, does not lessen the amount of fear the student feels. For example, most individuals who climb the pamper pole are scared of falling to the ground, and though the accident rate is very low on this element, the fear is still very real. When adventure educators use the word "perceived" in their brochures it implies that it is something the student is making up, and is therefore, not real. But, fear greatly affects one's emotions and can cause a tremendous amount of anxiety. To assume that students are only perceiving risk implies that it is solely a cognitive experience, however students do take their bodies with them which magnifies their fear. For these reasons the field should no longer assume that risks are perceived, not real.

It also appears as if adventure education programs are undermining the concept of "perceived risk." By stating that it is "more perceived than real" suggests that it is artificial, and therefore maybe not worth the effort. But, perceived risk is what makes adventure education so effective. People think they are in extremely risky situations, and by conquering personal fears, learn more about themselves. Therefore, this concept is an effective tool, which when used properly, has tremendous educational potential.

So why do some adventure educators assume that adventure education is only a perceived risk? They make this assumption because activities appear to be much riskier than they actually are. For instance, ordinary people observing someone on a ropes course high element such as a two-line bridge would consider the situation extremely risky. They would see someone high above the ground traversing a thin cable while connected to a narrow piece of rope. It appears risky to them, but to the instructors, who understand the breaking strengths of cables and ropes, as well as the safety procedures used, the risk of an accident is minimal. Most people don't realize how safe the equipment and procedures are. In fact, statistics show that adventure activities, such as ropes courses and rock climbing, are actually relatively safe.

For example, in 1986 Project Adventure Inc. conducted a 15 year study on ropes course safety and discovered a 3.6% accident rate per one million hours of use, and the majority of accidents occurred on the low elements which are usually less than two feet above the ground. For comparison, physical education classes in the public school system had an accident rate of 9.6% per one million classroom hours, and auto driving was at 60%. Furthermore, Ewert (1984), reports that adventure education is fifteen times safer than driving an automobile or participating in college football (p. 27-32). These studies prove that ropes courses, and adventure education activities in general, have a comparatively good safety record.

Nonetheless, it hardly seems correct, or for that matter fair, to suggest that adventure education is purely a "perceived risk." Some programs now give equal weight to both perceived and objective risk, recognizing that it is inappropriate to place all the emphasis on perception. The field of adventure education has an excellent safety record, but adventure programs cannot guarantee that all their students will have a risk-free experience. Instructors never have one-hundred percent control, and so risk assertions should give equal credence to both perceived and objective forms.

ASSERTION: "We'll challenge you to do your best and to accomplish more than you ever thought possible. This year discover your untapped potential..."(Outward Bound Revised Course Schedule brochure, 1991,p.1).

ASSUMPTION ONE: Individuals need to engage in physical challenges to tap their true potential.

Keyes (1985) suggests otherwise. In *Chancing It: Why We Take Risks*, he discovered that emotional risks such as falling in love, interviewing for a job, or talking in front of a group of people are more challenging than physical risks such as sky diving, rock climbing, or hang gliding (p. 41). This suggests that engaging in emotional risk-taking situations is just as effective, if not more so, at unlocking human potential than participating in physical risk-taking activities.

Rogers (1969) agrees. During an experimental college course he witnessed the benefits of emotional risk-taking: "Finally there was much risk-taking by the individual, both in expressing himself in a less guarded way, and in trying out new modes of interpersonal behavior, not only in the group but outside" (p. 75). People in Roger's class were taking risks, but on an emotional and interpersonal rather than physical level. Telling someone about your insecurities is one form of emotional risk-taking. You won't lose your life, but you might lose a friend or a lover. Another example is talking in front of a group: for some this is extremely risky because of the possibility of being rejected. Taking an emotional risk means doing or saying something that may cause you emotional pain. Disclosing very personal information, might mean risking embarrassment; or attending graduate school might mean risking failure. In either case your self esteem is at risk.

Yet the payoffs can be tremendous, as shown by the comments of one of Roger's students: "I value myself more as a person-my dependency needs, my anxieties, my proving needs, my inadequacies, and limitations, as well as my warm feelings for others, my knowledge, my competencies, my worthiness, my potential" (1969, p. 81). This student's reaction suggests that individuals could discover hidden potential by engaging solely in emotional risks without ever facing a physical challenge.

Moreover, how often do our daily lives require that we engage in physical risks? For the most part our daily lives do not require us to climb mountains or raft wild rivers, so wouldn't it make more sense to practice taking emotional risks? For example, rather than taking a 21 day Outward Bound course why not enroll in a program where participants have to expose their personal beliefs and values to the group? According to Keyes (1985), this is exactly the sort of thing we should do, because life consists primarily of taking emotional risks, and that is far more difficult than physical risk-taking: "No risk is avoided more often by taking even dangerous physical risks than that of looking foolish. In fact, much apparent "risk taking" is little more than activity engaged in to head off the greater risk of losing face" ( p. 168).

So why do many adventure education programs promote the use of physical challenges? They do so because physical risks place not only our body, but our emotions in a vulnerable state. For example, in Leroy's article "Adventure and Education", he describes how a woman on his Outward Bound course overcame her fears of climbing a glacier and how such an experience helped her become more courageous.

> *Priscilla's psychological adventure was monumental, just as deserving of acclaim as anything Amundsen did at the South Pole or Hillary did on Everest. And in turn, what those elicited emotions of Priscilla the conqueror (of herself) might in turn create are monumental in possibility. In fact, the creation of those emotions and all the potential for self knowledge and growth that accompany them is the reason for any adventure program's existence... (1985, p. 229).*

While most would probably agree that Priscilla's adventure was monumental for her, few would agree that it deserves the same adoration as Amundsen's or Hillary's accomplishments. Nonetheless, what Leroy is suggesting is that physical challenges are overwhelming because they put your life at stake. This creates a mental conflict which, when conquered, can lead to growth. In emotional risk-taking our lives are not at stake, but our feelings are; whereas in physical risk-taking our lives are at stake, or at least appear to be at stake, and often our emotions as well. And although we might not be worried about losing face while participating in a physical risk, we are worried about losing our life, which definitely heightens our level of stress.

This suggests that even though the two types of risk are different, there is at least one similarity. In both cases we must act in order to overcome fear, and to act in the face of fear requires courage. This means that courage can be developed by engaging in either type of risk. Therefore, adventure educators should not place all the emphasis on physical risks. Instead, they should challenge people to act upon their fears by presenting both types of risk.

Adventure education programs understandably place more emphasis on physical risks, but in reality emotional risks are as much a part of the learning process as physical ones. In fact, some programs such as Rogers Memorial Ropes and Challenge Course do not allow certain high risk takers the opportunity to participate on the high ropes course (Boeke, Lynch, Nies-Scargill, and Lee, 1988). They found that for many patients the low elements course, which requires more social interaction, was much riskier. In such cases, the risk is amplified because people are not only doing the activities but sharing their ideas and feelings with a group of strangers. When the perception of risk is no longer present, then the potential for growth may be limited. For instance, Keyes (1985) discovered that certain individuals thrive on physical risk and have no fear when doing certain activities. Petit, a famous tight rope walker, perceives himself in relation to his skill as a non-risktaker. He walks on cables high above the ground without any fear, and perceives himself as a non-risktaker because he believes he has eliminated all possible error. Individuals like Petit, who participate in adventure activities will not receive the same benefits as those who have to overcome the challenge of conquering their fears. This suggests that to optimize learning, participants should engage in activities that are perceived as challenging.

Since the term "adventure education" automatically conjures up images of hanging from cliffs and shooting whitewater rapids, it is important, especially for practitioners, to explicitly state that the adventure activities are only the means used to reach a greater end, which is intellectual, emotional, and spiritual growth. Too often the emphasis is placed on the physical adventure and the activity becomes an end in itself. If the goal of adventure programming is to truly tap potential, then adventure educators must work toward levels which go beyond the physical.

The following comments of Nold (1985), former director of Colorado Outward Bound, should be kept in mind by all adventure educators.

> *It is easy to be hooked on adventure. We have a distorted view of Hahn's vision, given the Outward Bound bias. Hahn valued the adventure ethic for the qualities of character it nurtured: self-reliance, self-sufficiency, endurance in the face of hardship, resilience. But he also harbored an underlying suspicion of Outward Bound. He was concerned lest it become a toughness cult or a haven for the wilderness freak, the social dropout (p. 55).*

An adventure experience can have a tremendous impact on a person's life. For some, one adventure experience is enough, whereas for others, it becomes a way of life. Some become so hooked on adventure that they plan their lives from one adventure experience to the next. Nold would agree that being hooked is not necessarily bad unless it limits growth. For instance, growth is limited or nonexistent when climbing instructors fail to provide their students with an opportunity to climb because they themselves are so obsessed with trying to improve their own climbing ability. In this situation the instructors are not concerned about promoting social responsibility or compassion, but instead are concerned only with themselves. When this happens, doing the activity becomes the primary aim and adventure education loses its potential to foster the students' personal growth. If the goal of adventure programming is to truly tap potential, then adventure educators must work toward levels which go beyond the physical.

ASSUMPTION TWO: We need external motivators (such as Outward Bound courses) in order to discover our true potential.

Some experts in the field of motivation would say we do not. Deci and Ryan (1985) developed a theory of motivation based on an organismic model where, "behavior is influenced by internal structures that are being continually elaborated and refined to reflect ongoing experiences. The life force or energy for the activity and for the development of the internal structure is what we refer to as intrinsic motivation" (p. 8). This approach suggests that motivation is not solely dictated by external factors, because there are many things we do simply for pleasure, or challenge, which have no immediate external rewards. For example, Deci and Ryan state that adults who are intrinsically motivated, "spend large amounts of time painting pictures, building furniture, playing sports, whittling wood, climbing mountains, and doing countless other things for which there are no obvious or appreciable external rewards. The rewards are inherent in the activity, and even though there may be secondary gains, the primary motivators are the spontaneous, internal experiences that accompany the behavior" (p. 11).

Opponents, however, argue that external motivators are necessary in order for us to discover our true potential. For example, Gardner (1961) discusses motivation, claiming that schools can achieve excellence and maintain equality by implementing tougher standards. He argues that: "We must understand that high motivation is as precious a commodity as talent and that if we do not have a system which selects for this attribute as well as for talent we shall have to resign ourselves to a good deal of flabbiness in our leadership ranks" (p. 100). Gardner implies that people are basically lazy and thus need external motivators in order to reach their full potential.

One must grant that this argument has a certain amount of credence. For example, I often hear college students during registration asking one another about easy teachers and which courses require the least work. They are not as concerned about receiving a quality education as they are with how to get by with as little effort and investment as possible. They want to know exactly what they have to do to get the grade they want. These students do *not* appear inherently motivated and seem to need external motivation.

And yet, if discovering our untapped potential involves learning how to overcome adversity, learning how to take risks, and ultimately learning about ourselves, then intrinsic motivation must be seen as a crucial ingredient. External factors can influence our behavior, and may even ignite the fire, but if there is no internal desire, learning will not occur. As Dewey warns, "In the strict sense, nothing can be forced upon them or into them. To overlook this fact means to distort and pervert human nature" (1916, p. 25).

From this point of view it does not seem possible to force someone to learn what you want them to learn, or to control the way in which they think. Learning is a process that takes place in the mind, and if one is not internally motivated to think, then one will not learn. Therefore, the initial impetus to tap our true potential must come from within, and once the impetus is present, the process of learning can begin.

> **ASSERTION:** "We are committed to live our vision of excellence by : Advocating the concept of challenge by choice." (Project Adventure, Inc. Workshop Schedule, 1993, p. 32).
>
> **ASSUMPTION ONE:** Individuals who attend adventure education programs have free choice.

Some behaviorists argue otherwise, and would claim that individuals attend and participate in adventure education courses because they are avoiding aversive stimuli.

Skinner (1971) argues that humans are creatures controlled primarily by environment: "A teacher threatens corporal punishment or failure until his students pay attention; by paying attention the students escape from the threat of punishment (and reinforce the teacher for threatening it). In one form or another intentional aversive control is the pattern of most social coordination-in ethics, religion, government, economics, education, psychotherapy, and family life" (p. 28). This statement implies that human beings do not have the freedom to choose their own course of action. In the case of adventure education, it suggests that students may attend because they are being controlled by external forces. For example, there are corporations who mandate that workers participate in adventure education programs. Workers realize that if they do not participate, it may cost them a promotion or even a job. Another example would be juvenile delinquents who attend Outward Bound courses so they do not have to serve time. In both examples individuals behave in certain ways because they are responding to aversive stimuli.

The same process often appears to be at work inside the programs themselves. For example, I have observed instructors screaming at students to complete certain adventure activities. In one incident the teacher would not lower the student to the ground until she had completed the climb. It was very obvious that overt force was being applied and that the student did not have much of a choice. In another incident, a well-meaning instructor was gently coaxing a student to continue negotiating a high element on a ropes course. It was clear that the student did not want to continue the activity, but the group and the instructor were able to apply enough pressure to convince the participant to complete the activity. In this situation the force applied was certainly not overt, but it was present, and it appeared that this participant proceeded with the activity primarily to avoid being embarrassed in front of fellow students. Such examples show that there are times when individuals make decisions which are not entirely of their own choosing, and that there are times when people are physically and psychologically forced to perform certain behaviors.

Opponents, such as the humanistic psychologists, reject this notion and believe that people have choice and freedom. For instance, Rogers (1989) uses instances from his work in psychotherapy to argue as follows: "What I am trying to suggest in all of this is that I would be at a loss to explain the positive change which can occur in psychotherapy if I had to omit the importance of the sense of free and responsible choice on the part of my clients. I believe that this experience of freedom to choose is one of the deepest elements underlying change" (p. 93).

Rogers implies that without freedom and choice, people exposed to aversive stimuli would always respond the same way. We know, however, that some individuals react very differently than others when exposed to the same aversive stimuli. For example, some individuals avoid participating in risk-taking activities at all cost, whereas others thrive on them. What is aversive to some, stimulates others. We cannot always predict behavior, nor can we control it.

Similarly, in *Man's Search for Meaning* Frankl (1959) describes the dehumanizing situations he experienced in a Nazi concentration camp. People were treated like animals; they were cold, hungry and starving, and many were ruthlessly exterminated. This caused many to give up on life, yet Frankl and a few others were able to psychologically overcome all these aversive stimuli. In reflecting upon his experience, Frankl states that, "everything can be taken from a man but one thing: the last of the human freedoms-to choose one's own attitude in any given set of circumstances, to choose one's own way" (p. 65). In this situation Frankl chose a proactive role. He decided to take control over his attitude and turn his experience into something positive. Aversive stimuli surrounded him, but he did not allow them to destroy his positive attitude.

Thus, while external stimuli may have the capacity to affect behavior by causing us to avoid some experiences and seek others, there are also internal factors at work. In *On Liberty* Mill (1859) describes human beings as needing freedom to act on their internal convictions. He argues that: "Human nature is not a machine to be built after a model, and set to do exactly the work prescribed for it, but a tree, which requires to grow and develop itself on all sides, according to the tendency of the inward forces which make it a living thing" (p. 123). These inward forces include a mind which first processes external stimuli and then determines how to act in a given situation.

In the case of adventure education, one can conclude that there are external factors which individuals process before determining whether they wish to participate in a given activity. For instance, on a ropes course students might conclude that their physical ability, the strength of the climbing rope, and the effectiveness of the belay procedure will allow them to safely participate in the activity. On the other hand, it may lead them to the opposite conclusion, and therefore they choose

not to participate. Finally, they may conclude that it is safe, but choose not to participate anyway. In all three of these situations there are external factors which play a part in the decision-making process, but ultimately individuals have the freedom to choose their own course of action.

However, just because adventure educators espouse the "challenge by choice" philosophy and tell people they can decide whether or not to participate, people do not necessarily choose freely. What appears to be a proactive choice may in fact be a reactive choice due to aversive stimuli. For example, while working at Rogers Memorial Hospital I encountered several patients who deliberately chose to misbehave while participating on the ropes course (Summer Ropes Course Program, Oconomowoc, WI, 1989). This in turn lengthened their stay at the hospital. I eventually found out that they chose to participate and misbehave on the ropes course because, once released from the hospital they would have to return to an abusive home situation.

Adventure educators assume that when they tell participants that they have free choice, the participants will indeed make a decision based on their own free will. This however, is not always true. If adventure educators truly want people to make free choices then they not only have to tell students or patients that they have a choice, but provide an opportunity for them to discuss their fears and concerns, which in turn will help participants become more aware of the choices they make. Adventure educators can never know with absolute certainty whether every individual is making a free choice, but by raising questions they can heighten awareness of this issue.

Finally, no one should ever be psychologically or physically forced to participate in activities that may be too challenging such as rock climbing, high ropes courses, or kayaking. Furthermore, individuals should have the right to decline from participation even during the course of the activity, as long as it does not put another participant at danger. This means they should be lowered to the ground on high ropes courses and rock climbs if they choose to, and stop paddling at convenient locations along a river. Instructors might think they know what is in the best interest of the student, and therefore try to manipulate them into participating, but only the student can truly know what is in his or her best interest. If adventure education believes that in order for significant learning to take place the individual must freely choose to participate, then participants should not be forced. It is the instructor's ethical responsibility to make sure that coercion is never used.

**ASSUMPTION TWO:** Individuals should have the right to decline from participation in any activity at any time.

This assumption is not true, especially when safety is a concern. There are certain times when participants do not have the right to stop their involvement. For instance, I once observed a middle school student unclip her belay device while belaying another student on a high ropes course. She thought the challenge by choice principle could be applied at any time during the ropes course experience. Obviously, she put her classmate at risk and should not be given a choice to stop the procedure in the middle of the activity. Catching someone during a trust fall, spotting on the low ropes course, and using appropriate safety equipment are other examples where "challenge by choice" does not apply.

Itin (1992) takes this issue a step further by suggesting that there may be times when instructors are doing their patients a disservice by allowing them an opportunity to opt out of an activity. He suggests that instructors may be acting as enablers when they allow patients to remain stuck in an old destructive behavior (p. 2). Rather than allowing them to back out the second they want to, Itin believes they should be challenged to explain their reasons for stopping the activity. This suggests that there may be times, especially with therapeutic applications, when participants should not be given an opportunity to back out of an activity without some discussion.

In summary, risk is an effective tool that can enhance personal growth, but when the term "perceived risk" is used it can give students the impression that the fear they feel is imaginary and therefore, insignificant. This is especially true of instructors who neglect to discuss the emotional impact of the experience with their students. People also get a false impression when they read statements which suggest that physical risks are the best way to tap potential. Physical risks are useful, but emotional risks can be just as effective at tapping potential.

Adventure education's views on human nature also have negative connotations. For one, it implies that people are lazy and need to be externally motivated. Adventure education may help motivate some, but it is not necessary for those who are already motivated. Secondly, these views suggest that people choose freely, yet in reality peers, colleagues, instructors, etc. may be making decisions for the participants. It is important to let people know they have a choice, but educators should realize that not everyone has total freedom of choice. Thirdly, instructors should be very clear when they explain the challenge by choice concept. Participants should have the right to decline from participating in an activity, but they should not be able to stop in the middle of an activity if it puts someone at risk of being injured. Furthermore, instructors should be aware that they may be promoting old behavioral patterns when they allow participants to back out of an activity the second they become scared. This is a delicate situation and instructors who have a background in psychology and therapy are best equipped to deal with such situations.

Adventure educators should work towards eliminating these misinterpretations. They should realize that risk is both perceived and objective, and that the student's perception plays an important role in the learning process. They should also recognize the importance of emotional risks. Physical risks create emotional stress which may initiate growth, however they may be detrimental for those who have an aversion to risk, or educationally void for "adrenaline junkies." Instructors should also understand that some people who enroll in adventure education courses are already highly motivated and do not need external pressure to discover their inner strengths. Finally, choice is an important component of the adventure experience, but instructors need to realize that external forces affect one's participation level.

## DISCUSSION QUESTIONS

- How do physical risks enhance the growth process?
- Explain the difference between perceived, objective, physical, and emotional risk.
- Is risk more perceived or objective in adventure education?
- Give some examples when adventure programs provide true risk taking experiences?
- Where does one draw the line between encouraging and coercion?
- Give some examples when students should not be given free choice while participating on a ropes course.
- Explain how these assertions reflect views on human nature.

## REFERENCES

Boeke J., Lynch, J., Nies-Scargill, P. , and Lee, S. Ropes and Challenge Program, Rogers Memorial Hospital, Oconomowoc, WI, 1988.

Deci, E.L. and Ryan, R. *Intrinsic Motivation and Self Determination in Human Behavior*. New York: Plenum, 1985.

Dewey, J. *Democracy and Education*. New York: The Free Press, 1916.

Ewert, A. The risk management plan: Promises and pitfalls. *Journal of Experiential Education*. *7*, 3, 1984.

Frankl, V. *Man's Search For Meaning*. Boston: Beacon Press. 1963.

Freire, P. *Pedagogy of the Oppressed*. New York: Continuum Publishing Corporation. 1970.

Gardner, J. *Excellence: Can We Be Equal and Excellent Too?* New York: Harper and Row Publishers. 1961.

Hale, A. Issues in challenge education and adventure programming. *Bradford Woods Journal*. Bradford Woods, IN, 1985.

Hunt, J.S. *Ethical Issues in Experiential Education*. (2nd Edition), Boulder: The Association for Experiential Education, 1990.

Hunt, J. S. Ethics and facility-based adventure education. National Ropes Course Symposium, Pecos River, New Mexico, 1990.

Itin, C. Challenge by choice as professional enabling. *Insight-Association for Experiential Education*. Fall, 1992.

James, T. The paradox of safety and risk. *Journal of Experiential Education*. 1980, Fall, 20.

Keyes, R. *Chancing It: Why We Take Risks*. Boston: Little, Brown and Co., 1985.

Leroy, E. Adventure and education. In R. Kraft and M. Sakofs (Eds.) *The Theory of Experiential Education*. Boulder: The Association for Experiential Education, 1985.

Mill, J.S. *On Liberty*. New York: Penguin Books, 1959.

Nold, J. On Kurt Hahn, John Dewey, and William James. In R. Kraft and M. Sakofs (Eds.) *The Theory of Experiential Education*. Boulder: The Association for Experiential Education, 1985.

Outward Bound Revised Course Schedule brochure, 1991

Project Adventure, Inc. Workshop Schedule Brochure, 1993.

Project Adventure, Inc. *15 Year Safety Study*, Hamilton: Mass., 1986.

Rogers C. *Freedom to Learn*. Columbus: Charles E. Merrill Publishing, 1969.

Rogers, C. Freedom to learn. in W. Noll (Ed.) *Taking Sides*. Guilford: The Dushkin Publishing Group, 1989.

Rogers Memorial Summer Ropes Course Program, Oconomowoc, WI, 1989.

Skinner, B.F. *Beyond Freedom and Dignity*. New York: Alfred A. Knopf, 1971.

Unsoeld, J. Education at it's peak. In R. Kraft and M. Sakofs (Eds.) *The Theory of Experiential Education* Boulder: Association for Experiential Education, 1985.

Unsoeld, W.F. Outdoor education. Lecture presented to Charles Wright Academy. November 19, 1976. (Olympia: Copyright 1979 by Jolene Unsoeld)

f  i  v  e

# AIMS OF EDUCATION

*The business of the educator — whether parent or teacher — is to see to it that the greatest possible number of ideas acquired by children and youth are acquired in such a vital way that they become moving ideas, motive-forces in the guidance of conduct. This demand and this opportunity make the moral purpose universal and dominant in all instruction-whatsoever the topic. Were it not for this possibility, the familiar statement that the ultimate purpose of all education is character forming would be hypocritical pretense... (Dewey, 1909, p. 2).*

The field of adventure education is no different in striving to create experiences that will better the human condition. In fact, Hahn created Outward Bound largely because he saw a society that lacked moral compassion (James, 1990, Skidelsky, 1969). This original idea still lies at the heart of most adventure education programs, however as the field became more diversified it expanded this idea and now includes more specific aims such as long lasting learning, teamwork, leadership, risk taking, cooperation, as well as moral development. The purpose of this chapter is to examine commonly held assumptions drawn from the aims of adventure education.

ASSERTION: "Yes, you'll learn some outdoor skills but you'll also learn a lot about yourself — things that will stay with you forever" (Western Canada Outward Bound brochure, 1991, p. 1).

ASSUMPTION ONE:  Students are truly learning things that last a lifetime.

Ewert (1990), who has studied the psychological affects of adventure education, suggests that the effects are not necessarily long lasting. In reporting on Iso-Ahola, Laverde, and Graefe's research, Ewert discovered that becoming more competent as a rock climber did not translate into feeling more competent in situations outside of rock climbing. He also concluded that, "an individual's level of self esteem will be more enhanced if they have had a day in which he or she has climbed at a very high level of competence and pushed his or her level of ability, rather than simply climbing at the same level time and again" (p. 56).

This suggests that simply participating in adventure education activities is generally not enough to have a lasting effect. First, the activity must be challenging, and secondly, in order for the experience to have a

lasting effect, feelings of competency about a specific adventure activity must be transferred to feelings of competency in general. This way students learn that they are not only capable of negotiating adventure activities, but that they have the potential to overcome other life challenges as well.

One thing adventure educators can do to increase the chance for successful, long lasting learning is to provide participants with an appropriate amount of challenge. Too much challenge will result in defeat or avoidance, and not enough will result in boredom. Dewey (1916) suggests that, "A large part of the art of instruction lies in making the difficulty of new problems large enough to challenge thought, and small enough so that, in addition to the confusion naturally attending the novel elements, there shall be luminous familiar spots from which helpful suggestions may spring" (p. 157). This means that the challenges should be large enough to create perplexity, but small enough so students maintain interest. It also implies that the challenges in adventure education should be incremental. Educators should start with easier activities and move to more difficult ones. This way the problems encountered from one activity can be applied to the next.

For example, instructors conducting one-day ropes course experiences may start with easy challenges, such as spotting someone doing a trust fall at ground level, and then move to a low element such as the Swinging Log. Eventually, students would work their way up to the high elements like the Incline Log and Pamper Pole. By using this progression "familiar spots" will be created, which can be applied to subsequent activities.

A second thing adventure educators can do is help participants make connections between the adventure experience and life in general. Gass (1985) discusses three ways that transfer takes place in adventure learning. The first is "specific transfer," where the participant applies one technique or skill to a different, yet similar skill. For example, after learning how to tie various knots for rock climbing purposes, the individual can then apply them to sailing. The second is "non-specific transfer," where one learns how to apply a principle in a similar situation. The skills necessary to solve an initiative problem, for example, can be applied to solving a math problem. The third is "metaphoric transfer," where an individual applies a principle from one experience to something entirely different. The challenges and rewards of climbing a mountain, say, could be applied to the challenges and rewards of writing a book. Without such

transfers adventure education can become virtually meaningless. This is why it is crucial for adventure educators to be aware of theory, and take an active role as a facilitator during group processing sessions so that transfers are made.

| | |
|---|---|
| ASSUMPTION TWO: | The learning that takes place in adventure education is more enduring than the learning that takes place in formal education. |

According to Dougherty and Hammack (1990) this does not hold true. They discovered that college students in formal academic settings learn valuable life skills and information about themselves that may impact them the rest of their lives. This type of learning that consists of such things as, general knowledge, civic and political attitudes and behavior, personal ambition, self confidence, and creativity, is part of the formal education experience, however it may not necessarily be part of the academic curriculum.

Interestingly, this is the same type of learning that adventure education programs promote. Certain research suggests that adventure experiences not only enhance self esteem, but has the potential to enhance self confidence, interpersonal skills, responsibility, and various of other characteristics (Kolb, 1988).

One of the main differences, however, between formal education and adventure education is that academic learning is usually the primary goal of most colleges, whereas personal development is the primary goal of most adventure education programs. For example, in adventure education the primary goal of a map and compass exercise would be learning how to effectively communicate and cooperate with the group, whereas in formal academia the primary goal would be learning the theory and practice of map and compass use. In adventure education technical skill is secondary to social skill as a learning goal.

Rogers (1969) also suggests that formal education can be highly enduring because it has the potential to change the individual's personality. The individual may become so engrossed with learning that both their intellect and emotions propel them forward in the process. This is similar to what can happen in adventure education. Some who engage in adventure activities start out shy and introverted, but by the end of the course or activity are assertive and extroverted. The experience actually changes the way they think about themselves and others. A change in personality can be highly significant and enduring, lasting a lifetime.

Learning about self is also important because in many cases it allows for more fruitful academic learning. Noddings (1984) discusses how important it is for the teacher to nurture nonacademic attributes such as self concept: "She cannot nurture the student intellectually without regard for the ethical ideal unless she is willing to risk producing a monster, and she cannot nurture the ethical ideal without considering the whole self-image of which it is a part. For how he feels about himself in general-as student, as physical being, as friend-contributes to the enhancement or diminution of the ethical ideal" (p. 179).

In this statement the monster she is referring to is someone who has no regard for emotional development. To stay clear of such situations she recommends that teachers work on enhancing the "ethical ideal" which is, "that condition toward which we long and strive, and it is our longing for caring-to be in that special relation-that provides the motivation for us to be moral" (p. 5).

For Noddings, emotional development is more important than academic learning because in the long run having a good self image is going to help the student more than knowing the multiplication tables. Furthermore, emotional development is foundational to academic learning in that students are more apt to excel in their learning after they develop a sound self concept.

Dougherty, Hammack, Rogers, and Noddings all suggest that this type of learning is enduring. It affects not only the intellect, but the emotions as well. It has the potential to change personality, which affects the way individuals look at themselves and the way they behave around others. When academic subjects are treated as separate entities without any regard for student interest, when there is no relationship between teacher and student, let alone a caring one, then formal academic learning will not be enduring. This means that formal education may be just as enduring as the learning that takes place in adventure education.

**ASSUMPTION THREE:** The most significant things one can learn are things about self.

Certainly, learning personal skills such as leadership style, ability to cooperate, and attitudes towards risk-taking are important, but there are other things we learn which can have just as much significance as the things we learn about ourselves.

Prochazka (1985), an experiential educator, suggests that learning how to learn is significant and long lasting. In "Internalizing Learning: Beyond Experiential Education" he describes several different levels of learning. The first is memorization, where, "information that enters the brain and is recorded for a short period of time before evaporating into the universe" (p. 174). At the second level students have some familiarity with the information, but are still unable to apply it. The third level of learning is more experiential in that students are using more of their senses and actually doing something with the information. The fourth level is the internalization level, where students begin to ask questions such as, "what can I create with this new information, how can I make it a part of my life and use it, and what can I choose to do differently now?" (p. 174).

It is at the fourth level that learning becomes meaningful and significant. By raising such questions students actually engage in a process of thinking, which, according to Dewey, entails the following steps:

*They are first that the pupil have a genuine situation of experience — that there be a continuous activity in which he is interested for its own sake; secondly, that a genuine problem develop within this situation as a stimulus to thought; third, that he possess the information and make the observations needed to deal with it; fourth, that suggested solutions occur to him which he shall be responsible for developing in an orderly way; fifth, that he have opportunity and occasion to test his ideas by application, to make their meaning clear and to discover for himself their validity (1916, p. 163).*

Becoming aware of this process and using it is not the same thing as learning about yourself, yet it has the potential to stay with you forever. Without it, students would have a difficult time making connections between what they learn on an adventure education course, and how they might apply it to their job or family.

They may learn that they have strong leadership capabilities and are able to consistently direct their group, but if they are not able to raise the types of questions that Prochazka mentions, then they have not learned to internalize their learning, and are therefore unable to transfer this learning from one setting to the next. In other words, learning how to learn is one of the most important skills one can attain.

Therefore, although people can and do learn about themselves during an adventure education course, they can also learn more about the process of learning. Adventure education provides a perfect forum to discuss this issue. On one hand, it offers an abundance of problem solving activities, and learning a process to address these activities will enhance one's ability to solve future problems. But it can also raise questions that help people learn about the process of learning: will more significant learning take place if the experience precedes the theory, are there some situations where theory must precede the experience, or does everyone learn the same way?

**ASSERTION:** "They have evolved from low, simple activities to the continuous element, high impact courses of today." (Challenge Designs, Santa Fe Mountain Center Brochure, p. 1, 1986).

**ASSUMPTION:** The higher the impact the higher the level of learning.

There is no doubt that an adventure education experience can have a major impact on a person. For example, participating in adventure activities such as a high ropes course requires that people climb high above the ground while connected to a climbing rope, and then negotiate certain obstacles or problems. They might climb to the top of a 30 foot telephone pole, stand on top, and jump out and away from the pole to catch a trapeze bar. This is not something one does on a day to day basis. It is extremely scary, requires intense concentration, and can take a lot of courage to jump for the bar. This combination of emotions can have a tremendous impact. When people reach the top of the telephone pole, they are usually too scared to talk, but after they jump and are caught by

the rope, they begin screaming and cheering. The experience is so powerful that people can't help but show their emotions. Almost everyone who participates on this element either laughs, screams, cheers, or cries.

But, will the amount of learning increase as the impact increases? Overcoming fear can no doubt help people learn more about themselves, and can also help people enhance their self esteem, but how much fear is necessary? For some, simply canoeing a section of flat water might be scary enough. They don't need to negotiate a class four rapids in order to heighten their self esteem. Furthermore, there is much learning which can take place simply by being involved in a group process. People have to communicate, negotiate, compromise, and cooperate, all of which lead to productive learning.

Unfortunately, not everyone in the position to develop adventure education programs understands this. For example, once there was a hospital administrator who, after experiencing a ropes course, failed to see the value of problem-solving initiatives and low elements. He wanted to build a course consisting of all high elements which would provide ultimate challenges for his patients. Developing such a course might help some students develop better self esteem, but for some patients the problem-solving initiatives are more challenging than the high elements. Both low and high activities have important benefits, and high ropes courses are not the only way to impact participants. The term "high impact" should not be equated with "high element."

Furthermore, the ropes course industry continues to develop new activities and elements that increase emotional output. Ropes courses are an artificial means of adventure, and they can be designed to increase the thrill factor. It appears that more and more courses are being built to increase participant fear. An example of this is the increased height of ropes courses being built.

There also seems to be a growing popularity of fear-inducing high elements such as the pamper pole, breathtaker, and squirrel leap. It appears that ropes course builders are trying to outdo one another by seeing who can build the highest and scariest course. What message is the field of adventure education sending out to practitioners and participants when so much emphasis is being placed on the high elements? What educational aims are adventure educators trying to achieve? Is their goal to scare people or educate them? If the goal is to scare participants then why not have them do a bungy jump or go on a roller coaster ride?

Rather than concentrating on the thrill factor, adventure educators should perhaps concentrate on the educational aims of high elements.

High events that utilize a dynamic belay system provide participants with opportunities to learn about trust and communication. Other high elements are specifically designed to enhance problem solving skills. But there are some high activities which are unique in that they do not require any problem solving or dynamic belayers. They appear to focus more on thrill than on education. For instance, the only thing necessary to accomplish the zip line or breath-taker is an able body. Such activities do not require any problem solving or trust in other students.

Adventure educators should think carefully about what they are trying to accomplish. If the only goal is to provide a thrill, then a day at the carnival might suffice. Adventure activities can be both thrilling and educational. The zip line and breath-taker, for example are scary activities, but they also have educational value. However, the educational value may not be as obvious as in some of the other adventure activities. Therefore, if one of the goals is to demonstrate educational value, adventure educators should be sure to emphasize the merit of each activity. Otherwise the opportunity for meaningful learning may be lost. If individuals are going to call themselves adventure *educators*, then they should provide programs which offer educational value.

> **ASSERTION:** "Outward Bound's professional development programs offer the perfect forum for developing the skills essential for success in today's world — teamwork, leadership, and risk-taking" (Outward Bound Revised Course Schedule brochure, 1991, p. 22).
>
> **ASSUMPTION ONE:** Adventure education promotes a willingness to take other risks once the student returns home.

According to Altham (1984) this may not always be true.

*One of the more evident facts in this area is that people's attitudes towards risk and uncertainty vary greatly. To some people, in some circumstances, the consciousness of risk has positive value. To others in the same circumstances, the consciousness of risk may be unpleasant. What gives one some pleasurable excitement gives another the pain of anxiety. A person may be temperamentally risk averse or risk loving. (p. 24)*

The fear of falling to the ground while rock climbing or negotiating a high element ropes course can become so overwhelming that it prevents some from continuing on with the activity. In extreme cases instructors have to climb up and actually help participants down. Such cases appear to promote resistance to future risk-taking. The psychological impact of such an experience could certainly lead to the avoidance of physical risk, and could even increase fear of any risk at all. Indeed, there are those who claim that participating in adventure will not increase their desire to take risks in the future.

For example, while teaching adventure activities, especially high ropes courses, I often heard statements such as, "the experience was fun and exciting, but really not useful to any other part of life" (Rogers Hospital Ropes and Challenge Course, 1988, 1989; Edgewood College, Issues in Education Course, 1989, 1990, 1991). Students who had participated on the ropes course claimed that the risk they experienced on a high element was much different than the risk affiliated with family or jobs.

ASSUMPTION TWO:   Adventure education experiences can be transferred to the work place.

One can argue that an adventure education course is vastly different from what one typically experiences at the work place. The surroundings are different, the activities are different, and the people are different than what you encounter at your work place. For instance, in an Outward Bound mountaineering course people are hiking in the mountains with a group of strangers, while many professionals work with the same individuals in an indoor setting day after day. The environments are completely different, so how can a transfer take place?

For one thing, there are certain characteristics common to both arenas. Participants in an adventure education program take risks when they voice their opinions to the group or climb a mountain, whereas in job situations people take risks when they challenge authority or experiment with new ideas. Communication is another example. To describe a possible solution to a problem solving initiative requires that participants communicate clearly, which is no different than the communication needed to solve problems at the work place. Even though the activities are quite different, the skills used to negotiate these activities are very similar.

Gass, Goldman, and Priest (1992) not only agree that certain characteristics can be common to both arenas, but offer specific ideas on how adventure education might be linked to the workplace. Their article, "Constructing Effective Corporate Adventure Training Programs," discusses four characteristics which help make corporate adventure programs successful. These characteristics are context, continuity, consequences, and care. Context refers to specific elements common to both arenas. Continuity links the learning that takes place during the adventure experience to future learnings at the workplace. Consequences refers to the idea that both adventure and work experiences can provide useful information and feedback. Care refers to providing a psychologically safe environment. All these characteristics, when implemented properly, can help individuals make connections between adventure education and their jobs. But although many skills can be transferred, adventure educators should not assume this will happen automatically. Adventure educators should highlight these skills and discuss their applicability so as to increase the chances that a transfer will be made.

ASSERTION: We are committed to...designing programs which help groups learn from one another and cooperate to develop healthy communities and environments" (Project Adventure Workshop Brochure, 1994).

ASSUMPTION ONE:  Cooperative learning situations are more effective than competitive ones.

According to Johnson and Johnson (1981) this is true. In one of their research studies on socialization and achievement they concluded that "the discussion process in cooperative groups promotes the discovery and development of higher quality cognitive strategies for learning than does the individual reasoning found in competitive and individualistic learning situations" (p. 146). They and their colleagues also compiled a review of 122 studies that examined achievement or performance in competitive, cooperative, and/or individualistic structures and found that an overwhelming majority promoted higher achievement in cooperative situations than in competitive or individualistic ones. Kohn (1986) agrees. In fact, he argues that competition is destructive and should not be used in educational and economic settings.

Learning by cooperating appears to be quite effective in adventure education settings. Groups work toward common goals when they do problem solving initiatives, plan expeditions, and climb mountains. They achieve these goals more efficiently when they listen to one another's ideas and then agree on a common course of action. When participants fully utilize the collection of ideas drawn from the group they become more effective at solving these problems. Working alone, which often happens at the outset of a program, typically takes the group much longer to solve problems. This suggests that when groups cooperate they are more effective problem solvers than when they compete.

**ASSUMPTION TWO:** Competition does not occur in adventure education settings.

As much as instructors may try to eliminate it, competition is inevitable in adventure education. Some groups want to know how they compare to other groups, and certain individuals immediately begin to compete against others in the group even though they are supposed to work together. Competition is so ingrained in our culture that adventure educators will have a difficult time eliminating it from their programs. Furthermore, there may be times when competition is useful, such as to motivate apathetic participants or to increase the amount of fun. I once had a group of adolescents who refused to participate in some initiative problems. Nothing worked, including bribes and threats, until I made it a competition between two groups. It definitely motivated them, in fact they were so inspired that they did the same activity over and over until the end of the session. Most of the time adventure programs will probably promote cooperation, however instructors should be aware that there may be times when competition is beneficial.

ASSERTION: "Our goal is to better society by enhancing the character and compassion of individuals" (Colorado Outward Bound brochure, 1991, p. 1).

ASSUMPTION:   Adventure programs can teach morality.

The field of adventure education has been claiming it teaches morality ever since the inception of Outward Bound, but can it actually make people better people? Durgin and McEwen's (1991) research suggests that morality is not necessarily learned or instilled in young people during an adventure education course. Their studies show that although positive behavior was exhibited by several students during the actual course, it did not continue after the individuals were placed back into poor family environments. Two conclusions they drew from this study were, "longer adventure courses might help more firmly establish desirable behavioral changes" and "it is absolutely essential that every adventure course for troubled young people be integrated with a follow-up support program" (p. 35).

On one hand, this research indicates that adventure education, at least for troubled youths, does not work, but on the other hand, the conclusions suggest that if it is to work, students need more opportunity to practice appropriate moral behavior. Morality is not something one learns in isolation, it must be practiced. As Aristotle observed,

*For the things which we have to learn before we can do them we learn by doing: men become builders by building houses, and harpists by playing the harp. Similarly, we become just by the practice of just actions, self-controlled by exercising self-control, and courageous by performing acts of courage. (1962, p. 34).*

Aristotle believed that morality, like any other skill, needed to be practiced if it was to be learned and perfected. The field of adventure education concurs. Students participate in risk-taking activities which require courage, and they work together in groups to overcome difficult tasks which require cooperation. For example, when on a group expedition students must communicate and function effectively as a group on a day to day basis if they are to achieve their goals. This process often results in a display of camaraderie and compassion.

Performance of these tasks has great potential for developing moral character, but, as Durgin and McEwen have indicated, one cannot guarantee that morality will be learned. Hunt (1985), professor of ethics at the University of Wisconsin, sums it up as follows: "The resources of the political means — authoritative commands and punishments — can make people do what the legislator wants them to do, but they cannot make them mean what the legislator wants them to mean by what they do" (p. 73). In the case of adventure education, instructors can provide people with experiences that allow them to practice being moral, but they cannot force students to perform them for moral reasons.

Finally, if adventure education's goal is to teach morality, then educators need to be aware that their own behavior can have just as much influence on the students' moral development as the curriculum itself. In *Moral Education...It Comes With the Territory* Purpel and Ryan (1976) suggest that students are exposed to a "hidden curriculum" and, "derive notions of fair play, justice and morality from how they are treated by the institution, its representatives, and fellow constituents" (p. 271). This implies that the teacher's personality, which is not a part of the formal curriculum, has tremendous potential to affect moral development. An instructor's demeanor and attitude can have just as much, if not more, impact on the student's moral development as the adventures themselves. Therefore, adventure educators should be aware that "how they teach" can have just as much influence as "what they teach." If an adventure program is trying to teach students courage through a rock climbing experience, yet the instructors are using psychological force to get the students to complete the climb, will courage be learned? In some cases it might, but in other cases it might lead to anger and frustration towards the instructor.

There are moral overtones behind everything we say and do, and if the primary aim is to teach morality, adventure educators must place as much emphasis on process as they do content. Moral education begins the minute students arrive for the course. In fact, it might have begun before that if the student contacted the school before registering. Therefore, adventure educators must constantly be aware of how they are presenting themselves to their students.

Teaching morality is not an easy task but it can be done. Adventure education has great potential in this area because it uses an experiential approach. Participants are faced with challenges which require action, and these acts are often compassionate, courageous, and just. But, even though there is opportunity for moral action, adventure educators cannot promise that everyone will learn morality. They can provide appropriate situations, but they cannot compel all people to be moral. Ultimately individuals will choose their own course of action. Lastly, adventure educators also need to be conscious of their own behavior. They should model moral behavior because their actions have just as much influence on students as the activities themselves.

In summary, the aims of adventure education are relatively clear: teamwork, communication, risk taking, leadership, personal growth, and morality. What is not clear is whether or not these aims are actually achieved. Numerous facilities, especially one day ropes course programs, claim that people can obtain these goals in a short amount of time. While there is potential for personal development, participants should not be led to believe that adventure education is a panacea. These are admirable goals that should be fostered in a program, but adventure educators should be realistic about what can be achieved in one eight hour day. To help promote positive experiences adventure educators should have a clear understanding of the goals, set realistic expectations, provide activities that truly challenge the individual, and make reference to these goals periodically during the experience.

## DISCUSSION QUESTIONS

- How is adventure education unique in providing transformational experiences?
- How transferable are adventure experiences?
- What type of impact is adventure education trying to achieve?
- When does competition occur in adventure education?
- When is cooperation unhealthy? When is competition unhealthy?
- Which is more effective at teaching morality — the activities or the hidden curriculum?
- Can adventure education provide something for all populations?
- Give some examples of how the field manipulates students.

## REFERENCES

Altham, J.E.J. Ethics of risk. *Proceedings of the Aristotelian Society.* 1984, *84,* 24.

Aristotle, *Nichomachean Ethics.* Martin Ostwald (Ed.). New York: Bobbs Merrill Co. Inc., 1962.

Colorado Outward Bound School Brochure, Denver, Colorado, 1991.

Dewey, J. *Democracy and Education*. New York: The Free Press, 1916.

Dewey, J. *Moral principles in education*. Carbondale: Feffer and Simons, Inc. 1909.

Dougherty, K.J. and Hammack, F.M. *Education and Society*. New York: Harcourt Brace Jovanovich, Publishers, 1990.

Durgin, C.H. and McEwen, D. Troubled young people after the adventure program. *Journal of Experiential Education*. 1991. *14*, 1.

Edgewood College, Issues in education class, Madison, Wi, 1989.

Ewert, A. Revisiting the concept of self esteem through outdoor experiential activities. *Journal of Experiential Education*. 1990. *13*, 2.

Gass, M. A. Programming the transfer of learning in adventure education. In R. Kraft and M. Sakofs (Eds.) *The Theory of Experiential Education*. Boulder: Association for Experiential Education, 1985.

Gass, M.A., Goldman, K., and Priest, S. Constructing effective corporate adventure training programs. *Journal of Experiential Education*. 1992. *13*, 1.

Hunt, L.H. On improving mankind by political means. *Reasons Papers*. Spr. 1985, *10*, 73.

James, T. The paradox of safety and risk. *Journal of Experiential Education*. 1980, Fall, 20. Hurricane Island Outward Bound brochure, 1991.

James, T. Kurt Hahn and the Aims of Education. *Journal of Experiential Education*. 1990, *13*, 1.

Johnson, D. and Johnson, R. The socialization and achievement crisis: are cooperative learning experiences the solution? In L. Bickman (Ed.), *Applied Social Psychology Annual* 4, 119-164. Beverly Hills: Sage, 1983.

Kohn, A. *No Contest: The Case Against Competition*. Boston: Houghton Mifflin Co., 1986.

Kolb, D. Self esteem change and mandatory experiential education. *Journal of Experiential Education*. 1988. *11*, 3.

Noddings, N. *Caring: A Feminine Approach to Ethics and Moral Education*. Berkeley: University of California Press, 1984.

Outward Bound Revised Course Schedule brochure, 1991

Prochazka, L. Internalizing learning: beyond experiential education. In R. Kraft and M. Sakofs (Eds.) *The Theory of Experiential Education*. Boulder: Association of Experiential Education, 1985.

Purpel, D. and Ryan, K. (Eds.) *Moral Education...It Comes With the Territory*. McCutchan Publishing Corporation, 1976.

Rogers C. *Freedom to Learn*. Columbus: Charles E. Merrill Publishing, 1969.

Rogers Memorial Hospital Ropes and Challenge course brochure, Oconomowoc, Wisconsin, 1991. Santa Fe Mountain Center Brochure, Santa Fe, New Mexico, 1986.

Skidelsky, R. *English Progressive Schools*. Baltimore: Penguin Books Inc. 1969.

Western Canada Outward Bound School Brochure, 1991.

s   i   x

# CONCLUSIONS

This analysis began by tracing the roots of adventure education back to the early writings of Plato. Through time ideas first stated by Plato and others were transformed into a theoretical basis for adventure education. Assertions reflecting these ideas were found in adventure education program brochures. These assertions raise questions concerning the theory and practice of adventure education. An examination of these questions led to conclusions on how to improve the theory and practice in this field.

One conclusion is that the learning process utilized in adventure education has the potential to go awry. The problem with this process is that at times practice is overemphasized and theory under emphasized. Adventure educators should be aware that it is important for participants to reflect upon and discuss their experiences so that they can be connected to future experiences.

Second, experiential education is not the same thing as adventure education. Adventure education is a sub-field that uses risk-taking activities such as rock climbing and kayaking. Experiential education, on the other hand, is a learning process which is initiated by perplexity or confusion, and is followed by planning, testing, and reflecting. This learning process is used by the field of adventure education, but adventure educators should not assume that participation in hands-on activities will guarantee learning. Hands-on participation is important, but for learning to occur the student must be engaged in the experiential problem solving process.

Third, adventure educators need to be careful how they portray risk to their participants. Risk is a part of reality, and objective risks such as lightning, avalanches, and rock fall cannot be controlled. The field of adventure education should not give people the impression that they can control all risk. Furthermore, risk is not *more* perceived than real. Any time someone ventures down a river or up a mountain, they run the risk of injury or death. Risk is not a figment of imagination, it is real. Therefore, risk is not more perceived than real, it is *both* perceived and real.

Fourth, adventure educators should not assume that everybody who participates in adventure education does so of their own free will. Court-ordered juvenile delinquents and corporate workers sent by their companies are examples of individuals who are forced to participate. Adventure educators can, and should, tell people they have a choice, but just because they make this statement doesn't mean people will participate freely.

Fifth, it is not necessary to participate in an adventure education course in order to tap one's potential. It is not necessary for people to overcome physical challenges to discover their inner strengths. For some the challenges of everyday life might be enough to discover untapped potential. Furthermore, if participating in difficult risk-taking situations is the key to tapping potential, then one should engage in emotional risk-taking activities, because emotional risks are more difficult to overcome than physical ones (Keyes, 1985). Adventure educators should not place all the emphasis on physical challenges. Instead, they should provide participants with the opportunity to explore both physical and emotional risks.

Finally, although the aims of adventure education are admirable, they are not always met. For example, programs which don't allow students to participate in the problem-solving portion of an activity are limiting rather than fostering personal growth. Developing skills such as teamwork, leadership, and risk-taking are other goals, which adventure education claims are essential for success in today's world, but there are some individuals who will not learn these skills and won't be able to transfer them to the workplace. Furthermore, not everyone is going to learn important life skills which stay with them forever, or become more confident and compassionate. No doubt these are important aims that adventure educators should strive to accomplish, but the field of adventure education should not give the impression that these aims will be accomplished, or that people will automatically be transformed into better human beings by taking a course.

Other, more general questions concerning the field as a whole can also be raised. For instance, who is adventure education catering to? Originally, it catered to apathetic youth. "Americans were overweight, deluged by material goods and technology; the young were seen to be increasingly apathetic and often violently self-centered" (James, 1985, p. 41). Today however, it appears that adventure education is catering to a variety of people. There are special courses for cancer patients, corporate executives, women, men, adults in transition, Vietnam veterans, adult children of alcoholics, people with eating disorders, and troubled youth. This suggests that adventure education can help fix broken psyches, empower the physically challenged, comfort people with terminal illness, restart stalled professionals, and enhance the wilderness experience.

A second question concerns what problems the field is trying to address. It appears from the brochures that adventure education can help eliminate problems with work, leadership, trust, stress, low self esteem, transition, behavior, drugs and alcohol, eating, or just life in general. Originally the purpose of adventure education was to curb moral decay, but today it helps people overcome a variety barriers. It is not just helping people become better people because many who enroll are already good people, but its helping them overcome physical and mental handicaps. It is helping people take control over their own lives.

Losing touch with our natural environment is another problem adventure education is addressing. At one time adventure, at least in terms of living in the elements, was a part of everyday life. We had to gather our own food, make our own clothes, and build our own shelters from what the environment provided. Today, we have isolated ourselves from our natural environment. Many of us live and work inside, and surviving in the wilderness is no longer an issue of concern. Yet, going into the wilderness can put us back in touch with our natural environment and ulti-

mately ourselves. Adventure education provides an opportunity to face physical challenges which were once a part of everyday life. It puts us back in touch with nature, and for many of us, that side of our being which yearns for adventure. It helps us, at least for a while, forget about our personal problems and concentrate on the essentials of life. It simplifies living, and gives us time to think about what's really important.

Another question is, can the field provide something for everyone? The skills learned at such schools as Outward Bound appear to be universal because everyone needs to know how to solve problems and cooperate in groups. Individuals also need to gain the confidence to take new risks and so continue to grow. Developing such skills can improve one's outlook on life, regardless of who they are. In this respect, adventure education has moved far beyond its primary goal of developing moral compassion, and has branched out to include a variety of skills necessary for improving the overall quality of life.

It seems that adventure education has the potential to positively influence every one of its participants. Its philosophy has always been based on helping people. It tries to build self confidence, enhance self esteem, develop better leadership skills, and help people learn to cooperate, while at the same time instilling a respect for the wilderness. In order to continue accomplishing these tasks, and to improve upon them, adventure educators need to be aware of the field's philosophy. They must challenge ideas which no longer promote sound educational practice. Commonly held beliefs about knowledge, reality, and morality should be examined on an ongoing basis so that theoretical ideas can be expanded and practices improved.

## REFERENCES

James, T. Sketch of a moving spirit: Kurt Hahn. In R. Kraft and M. Sakofs *The Theory of Experiential Education*. Boulder: Association for Experiential Education, 1985.

# BIBLIOGRAPHY

Altham, J.E.J. Ethics of risk. *Proceedings of the Aristotelian Society*. 1984, *84*, 24.

Apps, J. W. *Improving Practice in Continuing Education*. San Francisco: Jossey-Bass Publishers, 1985.

Aristotle, *Nichomachean Ethics*. Martin Ostwald (Ed.). New York: Bobbs Merrill Co. Inc., 1962.

Bambrough, R. *The Philosophy of Aristotle*. New York: The New American Library, 1963.

Boeke J., Lynch, J., Nies-Scargill, P., and Lee, S. Ropes and Challenge Program, Rogers Memorial Hospital, Oconomowoc, WI, 1988.

Brookfield, S. D. *Developing Critical Thinkers: Challenging Adults to Explore Alternative Ways of Thinking and Acting*. San Francisco: Jossey Bass Publishers, 1987.

Burton, L. *Critical Analysis and Review of Research of Outward Bound and Related Programs*. Rutgers University: 1981.

Cohen, S. and Rae, G. *Growing Up With Children*. New York: Holt, Rinehart, and Winston, 1987.

Coleman, J. in Keeton, M.T. (Ed) *Experiential Learning*. San Francisco: Jossey-Bass, 1976.

Colorado Outward Bound School Brochure, Denver, Colorado, 1991.

Crosby, A. A critical look: The philosophical foundations of experiential education. In R. Kraft and M. Sakofs (Eds.), *The Theory of Experiential Education*. Boulder: The Association for Experiential Education, 1985.

Deci, E.L. and Ryan, R. *Intrinsic Motivation and Self Determination in Human Behavior*. New York: Plenum, 1985.

Dewey, J. *Democracy and Education*. New York: The Free Press, 1916.

Dewey J. *Experience and Education*. New York: MacMillan Publishing Co., 1938.

Dewey, J. *Moral principles in education*. Carbondale: Feffer and Simons, Inc. 1909.

Dougherty, K.J. and Hammack, F.M. *Education and Society*. New York: Harcourt Brace Jovanovich, Publishers, 1990.

Drengson, A.R. What means this experience. In R. Kraft and M. Sakofs (Eds.) *The Theory of Experiential Education*. Boulder: The Association for Experiential Education, 1985.

Durgin, C.H. and McEwen, D. Troubled young people after the adventure program. *Journal of Experiential Education*. 1991. *14*, 1.

Edgewood College, Issues in education class, Madison, Wi, 1989.

Erikson, E. *Childhood and Society*. New York: W.W. Norton and Co., 1950.

Ewert, A. Revisiting the concept of self esteem through outdoor experiential activities. *Journal of Experiential Education*. 1990. *13*, 2.

Ewert, A. The risk management plan: Promises and pitfalls. *Journal of Experiential Education*. *7*, 3, 1984.

Farley, F. World of the type T personality. *Psychology Today*. May, 1986.

Frankl, V. *Man's Search For Meaning*. Boston: Beacon Press. 1963.

Freire, P. *Pedagogy of the Oppressed*. New York: Continuum Publishing Corporation. 1970.

Gass, M. A. Programming the transfer of learning in adventure education. In R. Kraft and M. Sakofs (Eds.) *The Theory of Experiential Education*. Boulder: Association for Experiential Education, 1985.

Gass, M.A., Goldman, K., and Priest, S. Constructing effective corporate adventure training programs. *Journal of Experiential Education*. 1992. *13*, 1.

Gager, R. Experiential education: strengthening the learning process. *Child and Youth Services*. 1982, *4*, 31-39.

Gardner, J. *Excellence: Can We Be Equal and Excellent Too?* New York: Harper and Row Publishers. 1961.

Ginsburg H. and Opper, S. *Piaget's Theory of Intellectual Development*. New Jersey: Prentice Hall, 1969.

Goldstein, K. *The Organism: A Holistic Approach to Biology Derived from Pathological Data in Man*. New York: American Book Co., 1939.

Hale, A. Issues in challenge education and adventure programming. *Bradford Woods Journal* Bradford Woods, IN, 1985.

Hunt, J. S. Ethics and facility-based adventure education. National Ropes Course Symposium, Pecos River, New Mexico, 1990.

Hunt, J.S. Dewey's philosophical method and its influence on his philosophy of education. In R. Kraft and M. Sakofs(Eds.), *The Theory of Experiential Education*. Boulder: The Association for Experiential Education, 1985.

Hunt, J.S. *Ethical Issues in Experiential Education*. (2nd Edition), Boulder: The Association for Experiential Education, 1990.

Hunt, J.S. Ethics. In J. Miles and S. Priest (Eds.), *Adventure Education*. State College: Venture Publishing Inc., 1990.

Hunt J.S. The philosophy of adventure education. In J. Miles and S. Priest (Eds.) *Adventure Education*. State College: Venture Press Inc., 1990.

Hunt, L.H. On improving mankind by political means. *Reasons Papers*. Spr. 1985, *10*, 73.

Hurricane Island Outward Bound brochure, Rockland, Maine, 1991.

Hurricane Island Outward Bound catalog, Rockland, Maine, 1996.

Issues in Education Course, Edgewood College, Madison, WI, 1989,1990,1991.

Itin, C. Challenge by choice as professional enabling. *Insight-Association for Experiential Education*. Fall, 1992.

James, T. Sketch of a moving spirit: Kurt Hahn. In R. Kraft and M. Sakofs *The Theory of Experiential Education*. Boulder: Association for Experiential Education, 1985.

James, T. The paradox of safety and risk. *Journal of Experiential Education*. 1980, Fall, 20.

James, T. Kurt Hahn and the Aims of Education. *Journal of Experiential Education*. 1990, *13*, 1.

Johnson, D. and Johnson, R. The socialization and achievement crisis: are cooperative learning experiences the solution? In L. Bickman (Ed.), *Applied Social Psychology Annual* 4, 119-164. Beverly Hills: Sage, 1983.

Keyes, R. *Chancing It: Why We Take Risks*. Boston: Little, Brown and Co., 1985.

Kneller, G. F. The relevance of philosophy. In J. Johnson, et. al. (Eds.) *Reflections on American Education: Classic and Contemporary Readings*. Boston: Allyn and Bacon, 1991.

Kohn, A. *No Contest: The Case Against Competition*. Boston: Houghton Mifflin Co., 1986.

Kolb, D. Self esteem change and mandatory experiential education. *Journal of Experiential Education*. 1988. *11*, 3.

Kraft, R. J. Towards a theory of experiential learning. In R. Kraft and M. Sakofs (Eds.), *The Theory of Experiential Education*. Boulder: Association for Experiential Education, 1985.

Kraft, R.J. Experiential learning. In J. Miles And S. Priest (Eds.) *Adventure Education*. State College: Venture Publishing, 1990.

Kurt Hahn Institute Brochure, Morganton: North Carolina Outward Bound School, 1991.

Kurt Hahn Leadership Center Brochure, Morganton: North Carolina Outward Bound School, 1991.

Leroy, E. Adventure and education. In R. Kraft and M. Sakofs (Eds.) *The Theory of Experiential Education*. Boulder: The Association for Experiential Education, 1985.

Little, T. History and rationale for experiential learning. *National Society for Internships and Experiential Education*. 1981, 1-13

Maslow, A. *Toward a Psychology of Being*. New York: The Free Press, 1962.

Mill, J.S. *On Liberty*. New York: Penguin Books, 1959.

Miles J. and Priest S. (Eds.) *Adventure Education*. State College: Venture Publishing Inc., 1990.

Miner, J.L. and Boldt, J. *Outward Bound USA*. New York: William Morrow and Company, 1981. National Outdoor Leadership School brochure, Lander, Wyoming, 1993

National Outward Bound Course Schedule Brochure, 1991

Noddings, N. *Caring: A Feminine Approach to Ethics and Moral Education*. Berkeley: University of California Press, 1984.

Nold, J. On Kurt Hahn, John Dewey, and William James. In R. Kraft and M. Sakofs (Eds.) *The Theory of Experiential Education*. Boulder: The Association for Experiential Education, 1985.

North Carolina Outward Bound brochure, Morganton: North Carolina Outward Bound, 1991

Outward Bound Revised Course Schedule brochure, 1991

Plato, *Plato's Republic*. G.M.A. Grube (Ed.), Indianapolis: Hackett Publishing Co., 1974.

Plato, *The Republic of Plato*. F.M. Cornford (Ed.), London: Oxford University Press, 1941.

Plato, *Theaetetus*. B. Jowett (Ed.), Indianapolis: The Bobbs Merrill Co., 1949.

Priest, S. The semantics of adventure education. In J. Miles and S. Priest (Eds.), *Adventure Education*. State College: Venture Publishing, 1990.

Prochazka, L. Internalizing learning: beyond experiential education. In R. Kraft and M. Sakofs (Eds.) *The Theory of Experiential Education*. Boulder: Association of Experiential Education, 1985.

Project Adventure, Inc. Workshop Schedule Brochure, 1993.

Project Adventure, Inc. *15 Year Safety Study*, Hamilton: Mass., 1986.

Purpel, D. and Ryan, K. (Eds.) *Moral Education...It Comes With the Territory*. McCutchan Publishing Corporation, 1976.

Richards A. Kurt Hahn. In J. Miles and S. Priest (Eds.) *Adventure Education*. State College: Venture Publishing, 1990.

Rogers, C. Freedom to learn. in W. Noll (Ed.) *Taking Sides*. Guilford: The Dushkin Publishing Group, 1989.

Rogers C. *Freedom to Learn*. Columbus: Charles E. Merrill Publishing, 1969.

Rogers Memorial Hospital Ropes and Challenge course brochure, Oconomowoc, Wisconsin, 1991.

Rousseau, J. J. *Emile or On Education*. A. Bloom (Ed.) New York: Basic Books, Inc. 1979.

Sakofs, M. Piaget-A psychological rationale for experiential education. In R. Kraft and M. Sakofs (Eds.), *The Theory of Experiential Education*. Boulder: Association for Experiential Education, 1985.

Santa Fe Mountain Center Brochure, Santa Fe, New Mexico, 1986.

Schoel, J., Prouty, D., and Radcliffe, P. *Islands of Healing*. Project Adventure, Inc. 1988.

Simmer, P. and Sullivan, J. *National Outdoor Leadership School's Wilderness Guide*. New York: Simon and Schuster, 1983.

Skidelsky, R. *English Progressive Schools*. Baltimore: Penguin Books Inc. 1969.

Skinner, B.F. *Beyond Freedom and Dignity*. New York: Alfred A. Knopf, 1971.

The Association for Experiential Education conference brochure, 1990.

Unsoeld, J. Education at it's peak. In R. Kraft and M. Sakofs (Eds.) *The Theory of Experiential Education* Boulder: Association for Experiential Education, 1985.

Unsoeld, W.F. Outdoor education. Lecture presented to Charles Wright Academy. November 19, 1976. (Olympia: Copyright 1979 by Jolene Unsoeld)

VanScotter, R. D., Haas, J. D., Kraft, R. K., and Schott, J. D. *Social Foundations of Education*. Englewood Cliffs: Prentice Hall, Inc., 1991.

Voyageur Outward Bound Brochure, Voyageur Outward Bound, 1991.

Weider, R. Experiential therapy: An adventure in self discovery enters the psychiatric hospital. In J. Miles and S. Priest (Eds.) *Adventure Education*. State College: Venture Publishing Inc., 1990.

Western Canada Outward Bound School Brochure, 1991.

Whitehead, A. N. *Process and Reality- An Essay in Cosmology*. D.R. Griffin and D.W. Sherburne (Eds.) New York: The Free Press, 1929.

Wichmann, T.F. Babies and bath water: Two experiential heresies. In R. Kraft and M. Sakofs (Eds.), *The Theory of Experiential Education*. Boulder: The Association For Experiential Education, 1985.

# ABOUT THE AUTHOR

Scott Wurdinger has been teaching adventure education since 1976. He has worked for a variety of organizations including Outward Bound, Adventure Based Experiential Educators (ABEE Inc.), Accessible Adventures, The Proudman Group, and The University of New Hampshire Browne Center; as well as psychiatric hospitals, and colleges and universities.

He holds a Ph.D. in Experiential Education (Union Institute, Cincinnati, Ohio), M.A. in Philosophy of Education (University of Wisconsin, Madison, Wisconsin), M.S. in Experiential Education (Mankato State University, Mankato, Minnesota), and a B.A. in Biology and Outdoor Education (Luther College, Decorah, Iowa). He has taught experiential learning and adventure education courses for Luther College (Decorah, Iowa), Mankato State University (Mankato, Minnesota), Edgewood College (Madison, Wisconsin), the University of New Hampshire (Durham, New Hampshire), and Ferris State University (Big Rapids, Michigan).

Scott is an active member of the Association for Experiential Education (AEE) and the Association for Challenge Course Technology (ACCT). He serves on the Journal of *Experiential Education* Advisory Council, and is on the Professional Review Committee for ACCT.

He is the Co-Coordinator of the Department of Leisure Studies and Wellness and Coordinator of the Challenge Course Program at Ferris State University.